C

A Play by
Michael C. Harris

**chicago** dramaworks

new plays. **chicago style**.

For my brother Chris, my father, and my good friends Sam Shepard, Albert Brooks, and Woody Allen.

# Characters
In order of appearance

RICH
CASSANDRA
SAM
ANDY
REBECCA
CHRIS
DAD
NURSE 1
NURSE 2

# ACT ONE
# SCENE ONE

*Interior of a well-appointed apartment living and dining room: stylish but comfortable furniture, bookcases teeming with books, an impressive entertainment center. There is a door leading into a kitchen stage left and a hallways stage right. There are tasteful painting and photographs on the walls. Successful professionals live here, and it looks like it. The phone rings, and the answering machine clicks on.*

RICH: Hello. Neither Sam nor Rich can take your call right now. Please leave us a message and we'll get back to you as soon as we can. If you are a telemarketer, please leave us your home phone number so we can be sure to call you back while you're eating dinner at home. Thanks.

*[BEEP]*

SAMANTHA: Hi Rich—it's me again. We *really* need to change that message. It's been on there for almost a year and it stopped being funny about 47 weeks ago. Anyway, it's about…10:30 here, so 9:30 your time. I just got in from dinner. Great Cuban restaurant. Typical dull work conversation, but really good food. One more meeting to go tomorrow. My plane gets to O'Hare right around six; maybe you'll surprise me by picking me up? I promise I'll surprise you. *(Pause)* Not what you're thinking, perv. I'll check in sometime tomorrow at your office. Don't forget that Andy and Rebecca are coming over for dinner on Saturday. Hopefully they were able to get a babysitter. *(Pause)* Well, nothing more here. Hope the concert was fun. Don't be too hungover tomorrow. *(Pause)* I miss you, Rich. These long trips suck. But I'll see you tomorrow. I can't wait. Bye.

*Phone rings again; answering machine picks up.*

RICH: Hello. Neither Sam nor Rich can take your call right now. Please leave us a message and we'll get back to you as soon as we can. If you are a telemarketer, please leave us your home phone number so we can be sure to call you back while you're eating dinner at home. Thanks.

*[BEEP]*

CHRIS: *(Shouting over loud bar noise)* Dude, you have got to change that stupid fucking message RIGHT NOW! I'm not hanging up until you change it. I know you're sitting there screening this call, you freak. It's me, Chris. What happened to you, Rich? We waited at the bar for you until show time, dude. Awesome show. *Awesome* show. Probably the best since we saw them in Milwaukee. Anyway—we're back here at the bar and I don't see you anywhere. You better be dead or in traction in the hospital. Talk to you tomorrow—I'll email you the set list I jotted down. Later. *(Crowd noise swells, then)* Oh Rich—did I mention that the show was *FUCKING AWESOME!* The rock was served tonight, bro. Later.

*As CHRIS hangs up, we can hear voices outside the door, keys jingling, fumbling at the lock. Door opens. Enter RICH and CASSANDRA. RICH is in his mid-30s and dressed in work clothes. CASSANDRA is in her mid-20s, darkly exotic looking—Indian? Italian?—with a suppressed voluptuous quality to her. She speaks with a Continental accent.*

RICH: ...it wouldn't be so bad if there were a few less assholes living here. But that's the deal with condos: everyone's an owner but they pretend they're just renting whenever something has to be fixed.

*CASSANDRA drops her backpack near the couch and crosses downstage.*

CASS: Wow. Great view.

*RICH puts his briefcase in its place by the door.*

RICH: That's what clinched it for us.

CASS: You really get the whole scope of the city.

RICH: It is a great looking city. Especially at night. It looks so...confidently urban.

CASS: "Confidently urban." Brilliant. There is something very matter-of-fact about this city. The architecture, the way it kind of pins down the lakefront. The people, too.

RICH: Considering all the cities you've seen and lived in...

CASS: *(Still at window)* Chicago's one of my favorites, definitely. It was one of the major reasons I decided to come here for med school. Every time our family visited here, my brother and I would just gobble up everything we could see of the city. He loves it too.

RICH: *(Heading toward kitchen)* Can I get you a drink? Beer, wine, water—

CASS: I'll have wine. No. Make that water. I need to take a little break, let my head clear a bit. My arms are already warm.

RICH: Love that warm wine feeling.

*Near kitchen door, he sees a wedding photo on the wall. He grabs the photo off the wall, glancing back to make sure CASSANDRA hasn't seen him, and heads into the kitchen.*

CASS: The wine was luscious.

*She begins looking at the photos on the entertainment center.*

CASS: Fantastic choice, Richard. *(Picking up photo)* I take it this is your ex?

*RICH enters from the kitchen with a beer and a glass of water.*

RICH: Uh, yeah. Yeah. That's her.

CASS: She's very pretty.

RICH: *(Handing her the water glass)* Yes she is. She is very pretty.

CASS: *(Taking the glass, with a smile)* Thank you.

*She takes a sip of water, staring at RICH, and then leans forward and kisses him deeply.*

CASS: Mmmm. Lovely.

RICH: *(Awkwardly)* Hard to beat a spicy Shiraz kiss.

CASS: True. So buttery.

*She kisses him again.*

RICH: *(Nervously)* A watery kiss is still pretty nice—as kisses go.

CASS: Very nice. *(Glancing around the apartment)* You said she's out of town, correct?

RICH: Completely. Very. New York.

CASS: *(Turning to look at the photos again)* It must be awkward still living here together.

RICH: Tell me about it. I don't even know why we—why I leave these pictures up. You'd think one of us would just put them all away somewhere.

CASS: How long did you say you were together?

RICH: Five years.

CASS: That's a long time for a relationship. *(Looking closely at one of the photos)* There are many memories tied to these photographs.

RICH: That's true. They're mostly good memories. At least the first few years. The past year hasn't been so great.

*RICH notices a picture on a nearby shelf and slides it into the books when CASSANDRA isn't looking.*

CASS: Why is it that it takes people so long to end relationships? I haven't had too many serious relationships in my life—haven't been in one place long enough, really. But even the one relationship I've had that lasted any length of time—

RICH: How long?

CASS: Almost three years. When I was at Cambridge.

RICH: That one went on too long?

CASS: Yes. At least a few months longer that it probably should have.

RICH: I think people just get comfortable in a relationship, and then when it starts going south, they're either too lazy to break it off or they're too afraid.

CASS: Exactly. I think it's fear. I think most people are so driven by fear—fear of hurting the other person, fear of being alone, fear of being embarrassed, fear of someone not liking them. So much fear ruling their lives that they become inert, unable to make a decision or take a stand or have the conviction of their own emotions.

RICH: So why'd it take a few months to end your relationship?

CASS: Fear. I admit it. I didn't want to hurt Matthew—that's his name—because he was a really sweet, sweet guy. Easy on the eyes, too. I liked having that steady someone around. I'd become accustomed to it as part of my everyday life. I was afraid of what it would be like to be alone again. Steady relationships have been rare for me, so letting go of that one was very difficult.

RICH: Who broke it off?

CASS: I did. Despite the fear, I felt I was lying to him every time I saw him, knowing that the relationship wasn't right for me anymore.

RICH: I know exactly what you mean. Every kiss goodbye, every head lean on the shoulder—a total lie on your part because you know you are just going through the motions.

CASS: Maintaining the premise that you're still a couple is a daily lie. It wears on you after a while.

RICH: I do think laziness plays into the equation as well. Humans are by nature sloth-like. But a lot less hairy. With way shorter tongues.

CASS: Speak for yourself.

RICH: But you know what I mean? When you first realize that you want out of a relationship—and you always know when it isn't right, no matter what mind games you play to convince yourself otherwise—your first action is not to break it up immediately. You put it off for a few days, a few weeks, a few months. See if things change...

CASS: Couldn't that be reasonable reflection rather than laziness?

RICH: Maybe a little. But I'm talking about when you *know* it's over. When you know you want out and are already considering worst-case-scenario exit strategies. That's when I think people get lazy. It's never a "good time" to reject someone's interest in you, right? *(Pause)* Frankly, I think it's as much the regular sex as anything. Who wants to abandon that even if you're not so hot about the relationship?

CASS: Ah yes. Sex is hard to abandon—whether it's regular or irregular.

RICH: Especially the irregular.

CASS: Sometimes the best kind. But I think that aspect of your laziness theory is particularly male.

RICH: If you're talking statistical averages, then yes, probably very male. But even now, with Sam and I breaking up, she kind of joked about "sticking around for the regular sex."

CASS: Who broke it off between you two?

RICH: Um…it was really mutual. Technically, I guess I broached the subject first. But we both knew it was over. She was trying to figure out how to end it and I was trying to figure out how to end it but not be a jerk kicking her out of here. I bought the condo, so she's the one who needs to move out. That's been the tough part.

CASS: When did you end it?

RICH: Four months ago—no, five. Five months ago. She travels a lot on business, so it's been kind of hard for her to try and find a place. In one way, it's good that she's not here much—we'd probably just get on each other's nerves.

CASS: It all sounds very civilized, though.

RICH: It is. But I guess that's the difference between a break-up when you're in your 30s and when you're in your 20s. Then it's all so serious. And dramatic.

CASS: *(Curtly)* Not for everyone in their 20s.

RICH: I didn't mean anything by it. I was thinking more about myself in my 20s. Everything—relationships, politics, family, music, friends—everything was *so important.* My essence was so tied up in every little thing. No sell-out, doing things my way, fighting corporate America, telling "the man" to fuck-off—you know, the typical ammo of a lucky middle-class kid all gassed-up on a liberal arts education.

CASS: *(Laughing)* It seems a rather virulent strain here in the States.

RICH: Do I hear another generalization?

CASS: No, not at all. There's just a stridency I see in so many Americans. Especially classmates. Like the world is at their feet. The assumptions they make! The entitled attitude they share. It's foreign to me.

RICH: Literally.

CASS: But do you know what I mean?

RICH: I do. Or I think I do, what with being born and bred here. In this country, we're raised with that attitude—that the world is ours for the taking. Whether you think it's good or bad or evil or whatever. I can't imagine growing up without having that…that—

CASS: Arrogance?

RICH: No. No, it's much more about freedom. The feeling that you really *can* do whatever you want. You grow up in this country with the idea ingrained in you that you can do or be whatever you set your mind to. You have nothing but choices—

CASS: Lots of kids I see on the South Side in my neighborhood don't seem to have so many choices.

RICH: True. You're right. *(Pause)* It's not perfect, granted. But even people in the harshest of situations here have more choices, more possibilities than in most places in the world. *(Pause)* Wow. I can practically hear "The Star Spangled Banner" playing in the distance.

CASS: *(Smiling)* You wear your ethnocentrism quite well. Sexy, even.

RICH: Thank you. I think. I should take that as a compliment?

CASS: Absolutely. I didn't mean to hassle you about this country-it's probably where I'll end up living. It truly is the most open and free place I've ever been. Or lived.

RICH: *(Going to stereo)* It strikes me maybe just a wee bit rich for the daughter of a diplomat to be casting aspersions on our little American dream.

CASS: Well played—I stand accused. Though Italy is not one of your super powers these days.

RICH: Oh. So it was only a little bit of privilege then? Your chauffeur drove a Lincoln instead of the full-on limo.

CASS: No need to get sassy about it. I'll have you know that for most of his career in foreign service, my father drove his own car, thank you very much.

RICH: Then we do have something in common. My dad drives his own car too. Though mostly to chauffer his new wife around.

CASS: His new wife? Not your mother I presume?

RICH: Correct. My parents got divorced about 10 years ago. You don't mind if I put some music on, do you? I've got "Oh say can you see" running through my head ever since that flag-waving episode a few minutes ago.

CASS: Please do. Do your parents get along now?

RICH: They get along all right. They don't really cross paths much. My mom moved out to San Francisco a number of years ago. There are no grandkids or anything for them to both need to be in the same place. How about your folks?

*Music starts: John Coltrane's "Favorite Things."*

CASS: My mother died a few years ago. Cancer.

RICH: Sorry I asked.

CASS: Don't be. It was lung cancer. She smoked.

RICH: It's a terrible way to go.

CASS: It went very fast—for her sake. They found it in her lungs in the summer and she was gone before Christmas.

RICH: I'm really sorry, Cassandra.

CASS: She was very aware of what she was doing, my mother was. Very smart woman. Not about her health, obviously. But she took a very...very existential view of the whole thing. "I chose to smoke," she'd say, "because I liked it. I knew it would probably kill me—and now it is." She wasn't surprised. She said she liked her odds. Her father smoked and he lived to be 97. My mom was 56. She said she thought the odds were better...

RICH: I don't mean to sound like a jerk here, but I couldn't help notice that you—

CASS: Smoke too? I was wondering how long it would take for you to mention that. Very kind of you to wait a few seconds. *(Pause)* I know it makes absolutely NO SENSE. I can't explain why I do it. It's stupid. And I don't like the odds at all.

RICH: You can always quit, right?

CASS: I will. I should. Not only because it's so stupid, but it's even more dangerous to smoke when you're on the pill. I've got lung cancer and blood clots waiting for me in every pack. Every drag.

RICH: You said she was from—

CASS: Egypt. From a very well-to-do Cairo family. Very high caste, but quite progressive. My mother and her sisters were all well educated, which was not normal when she was growing up. Even though my father is from a very esteemed family in Florence, and was well-educated and already beginning his career in the foreign service, there was a little looking down the nose at him from my mother's family. My grandmother especially. She never did come around to my father.

RICH: In-laws are tricky things. Especially mother-in-laws. *(Catching himself)* At least that's what my married friends tell me.

CASS: My mother and grandmother had a very odd relationship. Almost competitive, I always thought. They were so much alike— "due muli testoni" my grandfather used to call them. Two stubborn mules. I've got a little bit of that from them, I know.

RICH: So it's genetic.

CASS: Perhaps. My mother brought me up to not take shit from anyone—even her sometimes. She was the one to draw the line in the sand when my father wouldn't. Or couldn't. He's a politician, after all. He's all about negotiation and finding the middle ground. Luckily I get some of that from him, too. *(Changing the subject)* So, what about your family? Why did your parents divorce?

*Phone rings. RICH looks at it from across the apartment. The answering machine clicks on. As the message plays, he moves casually toward the phone.*

RICH: Hello. Neither Sam nor Rich can take your call right now. Please leave us a message and we'll get back to you as soon as we can. If you are a telemarketer, please leave us your home phone number so we can be sure to call you back while you're eating dinner at home. Thanks.

*[BEEP]*

CASS: *(Laughing)* That's really funny.

SAM: Hello again. It's me. I almost forgot—you need to call Dad and ask him if I can still borrow his—

*RICH turns the volume down on the machine.*

RICH: Don't need to hear all that.

CASS: I didn't think people still had those machines.

RICH: It's totally old school. But they're coming back—like vinyl. Just you watch.

CASS: Was that your ex? What's her name again?

RICH: *(Heading back to kitchen, trying to be casual)* Sal. Sally—people call her Sal. She's wants to borrow this thing from my dad for this work thing she has.

CASS: That must be a little awkward. For you, I mean.

RICH: *(From kitchen)* Maybe a little. But they get along—got along really well.

CASS: Apparently, if she's borrowing something from your father.

*RICH returns with two beers, handing one to CASS.*

RICH: They do get along. My dad thinks I'm an idiot for breaking up with Sam—*SAL.* He thinks I'm the one who broke things off.

CASS: I thought you said you were the one?

RICH: Officially. Technically, yes, it was me. But like I said—it was mutual. We both agreed that it was the best thing to do. But try explaining that to your parents. What were we talking about before the phone—?

CASS: Divorce. Why your parents divorced.

RICH: That's right. Boring story. They got married way too young, when they were 19 and 20. Had kids right away—my brother and I—and then after we got into high school and college, they realized they didn't really even know each other anymore. And then as they got reacquainted, they found they weren't the same people anymore. Weren't really interested in staying with each other. Kind of a recurring story with lots of people. Lots of parents.

CASS: It's still too bad. Still sad.

RICH: It was truly for the best. They both agree on that. But my mom had a little habit...not really a habit, not regular like a habit... *(searching for words)* let's just say my mom had a few extra-marital dalliances over the years.

CASS: Ah. There's the heart of it. A few?

RICH: I guess there were more than one or two. I don't really know all the details. Don't know if I ever really wanted to know the details. If you ask my father why they got divorced, it was because they grew apart. Doesn't even mention the...

CASS: Affairs?

RICH: Such an ugly word.

CASS: But it's what they were, right?

RICH: I don't even know. "Affair" means something prolonged, covert, sneaking around for months or years in scummy hotel rooms.

CASS: They don't have to be in "scummy" hotel rooms.

RICH: True. It's the sneaking around for a long stretch of time— that's the part of the word "affair" that bothers me. In referring to my parents' marriage anyway. People in movies have "affairs." Not your parents.

CASS: What does your mom refer to them as?

RICH: My mom never talks about it. The couple of times she ever even alluded to the subject she referred to "a few meaningless incidents." That was her word: "incidents."

CASS: Fair enough.

RICH: My mom told me one time that she's pretty sure my father never really forgave her for those...incidents.

CASS: I thought you said they both agreed it was for the best? Their divorce, I mean.

RICH: They do. Now. My dad wasn't so keen on it at first. I think it took him a couple of years before he really felt that it was the only real solution. It was very clear to my mom and my brother at the time.

CASS: Is that your brother—the one in the tuxedo in that picture there?

RICH: *(A little startled)* Yeah. Yeah that's him. Chris.

CASS: He's older?

RICH: Yep. Four years.

CASS: *(Picking up the picture)* There's a resemblance alright.

RICH: He looks more like my dad—a lot like my dad, in fact. I'm more a mix of my parents.

CASS: *(Gesturing to picture)* His wedding?

RICH: No. No, he's not married. Decidedly not married. That was taken at my dad and his new wife's wedding.

CASS: Does his new wife have a name?

RICH: Alice. They got married a few years ago. They dated for years. "Courting" is how my dad referred to it. Kinda old fashioned.

CASS: It sounds sweet. Nothing wrong with a little old fashion courting.

RICH: Nothing at all. But what really struck me about my dad at that time was how this old-fashioned attitude he held was like another layer of his personality that was new to me. I had to adjust my idea of him a little bit. It made me understand him in a new way.

CASS: I think everyone goes through that with their parents as they get older.

RICH: Definitely, but I was a little more oblivious to a lot of it. Certainly more so than my brother. It wasn't until I was in my 20s, when my parents were going through their divorce, that I learned of these trysts my mom had over the years.

CASS: Trysts! That's a great word for it.

RICH: Just thought of it. But I find out from my brother that he'd known about it since he was like 13 years old. When one of them happened.

CASS: You said your parents didn't talk about it.

RICH: They didn't. But I never even considered that it could happen with them. In the couple of years before my parents split up, I knew things weren't good between them, but I didn't really think they'd get divorced. One day my brother and I are out at this street fair watching this band and he asks me "so do you want to put any money on who files for divorce?" I had no idea who he was talking about. "I mean mom and dad," he said. He was so certain.

CASS: Who'd you put money on?

RICH: My dad. We bet a dollar.

CASS: And?

RICH: I lost. But Chris later revealed that he had a little inside info on the situation. Apparently my mom had been talking to him about some of the problems she and my dad were having. My parents tend to talk to Chris about their personal stuff more than they do to me. Especially my mom. I'm her "baby," so even though I'm a grown adult, she still holds on to a little of that attitude. Doesn't want to worry me about things—that kind of crap. My dad's a little more open with me about things.

CASS: So your mom told your brother she was going to file for divorce? Before he made the bet?

RICH: No—she didn't say anything outright. Chris said he kind of put it together from things my parents had said to him, they way they acted toward each other. I sure as hell didn't put it together. I really just thought they were going through a rough patch. Like all married couples.

CASS: My brother's like that too. He picks up on those kinds of subtleties better than I do. He's older, two years. It's like he's more attuned to the subtext of things. I wish I was more attuned to that stuff.

RICH: Me too. I just don't think that way. I don't want to sound stupid here, or surfacey, but I pretty much take people at their word. It's naive, I know. Chris says it's because I'm too innately honest. He says I don't read too deeply between the lines because I don't play those kinds of games myself. Which I think is true.

CASS: But that's a good thing. *(Pause)* At least I think it is.

RICH: I do too. There's enough going on in my life that I don't have the time or energy to play those kinds of mind games. But I just wish I was the one who perceived something first sometimes. I'm usually the one you have to fill in after the fact.

CASS: *(Moving to RICH on the couch)* I'll choose to remain slightly naive, I guess. It's worked for me so far.

RICH: Me too.

CASS: I could never lie to my parents as a kid—they always knew.

RICH: Tell me about it. I'd be a total failure as a spy.

CASS: But neither could my mother. She was extremely direct. Awkwardly so, sometimes. She could really read people, though. She bailed my father out of plenty of sticky situations over the years.

RICH: My mom's pretty direct, too. She's the type of person who says things like "Who did that to your head?" after you get a bad haircut. Not a lot of sugarcoating with mom.

*CASS grabs RICH's arm to read his watch.*

CASS: It's getting late.

RICH: Yeah. For a school night.

CASS: Can I stay and finish my beer?

RICH: Yeah, yeah. Of course. No rush.

CASS: *(Smiling at him)* Did you read that?

RICH: What?

CASS: I asked if I could stay and finish my beer.

RICH: *(Not really getting it)* Oh. Gotcha.

CASS: *(Laughing)* You don' get it. I don't even get it.

RICH: Well, truth be told...

CASS: I can't even speak between the lines effectively. It made no sense. What a sorry attempt.

RICH: Attempt at what?

CASS: Attempt at this. *(She kisses him)* Flirting's not my forte.

RICH: Not mine, either.

CASS: *(She kisses him again)* This is much more to the point.

RICH: Direct. Yes. Perfectly clear.

*They kiss again, more passionately, their bodies pressing closer together on the couch.*

RICH: So the beer finishing line was your lead-in?

CASS: *(Blushing slightly)* I know, I know. It didn't make any sense at all.

RICH: Oh I got it alright.

*Another long kiss.*

CASS: Tocca me.

RICH: *(Slightly breathless)* What was that?

CASS: Italian. Tocca me. *(Kiss.)* Touch me.

RICH: My Italian's a little rusty.

*He tentatively touches her arms, face, hair…*

CASS: *(Breathily)* Mas. Tóqueme mas.

RICH: More Italian?

CASS: Spanish. And more, yes.

*She takes his hand and places it near her breast.*

RICH: I knew I should have studied a second language…

*Coltrane swells. Fade to black.*

## SCENE TWO

*Lights come up on RICH and SAMANTHA, ANDY and REBECCA, seated at the dining room table. They have finished dinner and are lingering over wine and coffee.*

SAM: I'm not surprised that they're getting divorced, that's for sure. I've known Colleen since college and she's notorious for hooking up with the wrong guy—

ANDY: There's nothing "wrong" with Kevin.

RICH: At least not physically. That we can see.

REBECCA: He's an oddball. I can't remember having even one reasonably normal conversation with him in the past—how long have they been together? Six years?

ANDY: Be fair. Colleen's freaky in her own right.

SAM: Very freaky. She always has been, as long as I've known her.

ANDY: I mean, she literally dated carny people for a while there—

SAM: Carny *person*. It was one guy. And he booked the shows.

ANDY: Yes, but his aunt was the bearded sword-swallower. Had an 11th finger, too. Those were his "people."

REBECCA: At least that guy—what was his name? Rudolpho or something? At least he was interesting to talk to and could maintain a normal conversation.

RICH: Eduardo—Eduardo Sabatini.

SAM: That's right: *(dramatically)* Eduardo.

ANDY: Kevin was a trip. *Is* a trip to talk to.

REBECCA: I always got the feeling that he was vaguely hitting on me.

ANDY: You think most men are "vaguely" hitting on you.

REBECCA: That's not true. But he said some really suggestive things to me.

ANDY: Such as?

REBECCA: I told you about that time he asked me if I knew what a camel toe was.

*RICH almost sprays the table with wine.*

ANDY: You were wearing those freaking bike shorts. He was trying to be polite, I think. In his weird way.

RICH: *(To Rebecca)* What did you answer?

ANDY: She didn't know what he meant.

REBECCA: That's not the point. It was a weird thing to ask one of your wife's friends.

SAM: That sounds like Kevin all right.

REBECCA: *(To Sam)* Do you know what a camel toe is?

SAM: Oh yeah. Too much information. We've all been there.

REBECCA: *(To Andy)* And why the hell was he staring at my crotch anyway, huh?

ANDY: Because, Rebecca, when you wear those biking shorts, it's like an advertisement. Or an X-ray.

REBECCA: That's *my* problem. *He* shouldn't have been staring at my crotch.

ANDY: *(Frustrated)* Ugh. Ask Rich. You've seen her wear those shorts?

RICH: I have indeed.

ANDY: And?

RICH: And what?

ANDY: Camel toe?

RICH: I have no idea what you're talking about.

SAM: Correct answer.

ANDY: You're full of shit.

REBECCA: See? Kevin's a perv. A weird, freaky, oddball perv.

*RICH stands and starts to clear dishes from the table.*

RICH: I wouldn't notice your crotch anyway, Rebecca. I'd be too busy staring at your rack.

REBECCA: *(Laughing)* I can live with that.

RICH: But as to Kevin the perv, I want to go on record as saying that, despite his apparent obsession with Rebecca's crotch—which is all he ever talked about—

SAM: *(Joining in)* He was asking *me* about it all the time.

ANDY: I'm her husband and he called me about it countless times.

REBECCA: Alright already.

RICH: Yes. Despite Kevin being an oddball—

REBECCA: And a perv.

RICH: And an alleged perv, and the fact that we all know Colleen's strange in her own right, I think it's too easy for us to sit here and analyze them and make our pithy comments when we really don't know what goes on between two people in their marriage.

REBECCA: Don't get all reasonable on us now.

SAM: Yeah—you're taking the fun out of this. Of course we don't know the intimate details of their marriage, but that's the fun of speculating, right?

REBECCA: Absolutely. No harm done.

RICH: They were an odd couple alright, and I really have no idea why they even got married to begin with, but I always figure other people wonder the same thing about us *(gestures to Sam)*. Who am I to pass judgment?

ANDY: Now that you've broached the subject...

SAM: *(To Rich)* But you never ask people those kinds of personal questions anyway.

RICH: *(Going to kitchen with dishes)* I usually don't—because it's none of my business. If someone wants to tell—

SAM: *(Finishing his sentence)* "Me something, I figure they will." That's why you never get any good dish, Rich. You gotta ask.

REBECCA: What's the harm in asking, right?

ANDY: I know what Rich is talking about. I think it's the way men are brought up—not to ask people personal questions. Especially not to other men.

RICH: *(From kitchen)* It's like an unwritten law that you don't question or comment or get catty about a friend's wife. Or girlfriend.

ANDY: It's true. Even if you think they're completely insane. Or a hideous ogre.

SAM: But they're your friends. If you can't talk about personal stuff with friends, who can you talk to?

RICH: *(Returning to table)* You can talk about personal stuff. I talk to my brother, my dad, Andy here—

ANDY: It's not that you *can't* talk about really personal stuff with other men, it's just that we're not really all that good at it.

REBECCA: That is the truth.

ANDY: *(To Rebecca)* See, with you it's different. It's part of the deal, part of what men are raised to expect. You can talk to your wife or girlfriend about how you feel. They're the safe zone. Sometimes you can talk to your sister, maybe even your mom. But you don't necessarily turn to the guys you hang out with. We hardly know the language.

REBECCA: I think that's true. Historically women have always been the communication line in families, between families—

SAM: I'm not dismissing what you're saying, Andy—that men aren't really raised in our culture to express their feelings—

ANDY: And *women*, from the time they're girls, are allowed to be more emotionally expressive than—

RICH: Thus they learn "the language," as you referred to it.

SAM: I agree, but I guess what frustrates me is that people have been talking and writing about this for decades now, yet it doesn't seem to be getting any better.

RICH: *(Returning to kitchen with dishes)* I don't know. I don't think men like my father or men of his "baby boom" generation still live with that very closed—

SAM: Rich, your father's not a good example.

ANDY: But it's still a valid point. Take my father—

REBECCA: Please.

ANDY: Ba-DUM-bum! He's a better example. Very stoic. Very closed. Super nice guy, really warm, friendly—the kind of guy you meet and really like. But try to talk to him about personal, emotional things? Forget it.

REBECCA: I'll never forget how teary-eyed he got in the hospital when he first held David.

SAM: That was his first grandchild, right?

REBECCA: Yes. And he sat in the chair in that hospital room holding David and just stared at him for like an hour. Hardly said a word—just grinned from ear to ear with watery eyes.

ANDY: But that's what I mean. He didn't verbalize his feelings. Maybe he did to my mom—

REBECCA: He was very sweet, Andy. He was so proud.

ANDY: Yes, but I have to believe he was feeling complex emotions at the time but he didn't know how to express them. He'd never really learned the vernacular.

REBECCA: Maybe there has been progress, Sam. Because Andy was a flat-out blubbering mess when David was born.

*RICH returns to the dining room with a coffee pot.*

RICH: Ah! See? His stoic dad was "sweet," yet Andy's genuine emotional reaction to the birth of his son was "a blubbering mess."

REBECCA: Oh come on, Rich.

RICH: *(Filling coffee cups)* Come on nothing. It makes a point. The same way men are raised to bottle their emotions, or at least play it extremely close to the vest, women have been ingrained with this idea that men who are overtly emotional are somehow weak.

SAM: Now that is a gross generalization.

*SAM picks up her coffee and walks toward the sofa.*

ANDY: Geeee-ross.

SAM: And over-simplification.

RICH: O.K. It's a little sweeping, but I think the point is legitimate—

REBECCA: *(Standing to join SAM on the sofa)* I think that's an argument for men to continue to be emotionally distant. It's a cover.

ANDY: It's not a cover. It's a fact. You can't deny that it's an ingrained cultural fact.

SAM: It may be a regrettable fact of the culture, but it doesn't mean men have to blindly perpetuate it. You do have a choice you know.

RICH: I'm just saying that a lot of men are raised with a really shallow palette of emotions they are allowed to feel. That are O.K. for boys to feel. Or talk about.

SAM: Anger is a biggie.

RICH: Yes—that one's sanctioned.

ANDY: You can get pissed and yell and throw things—from a very young age.

SAM: Pride. Pride's another biggie.

REBECCA: *Stupid* pride's a biggie.

ANDY: Women do stupid pride too.

RICH: Happiness. But once you get to a certain age, not too much happiness. None of that silly tears happiness.

ANDY: Indignation. Which is connected a bit to pride, I think. Righteous indignation is fair game.

RICH: Excitement—but again, only so much excitement.

ANDY: I'm tapped. Anybody else?

SAM: Perpetual horniness?

REBECCA: *(Laughing)* That's more like breathing than an emotion, isn't it?

RICH: Very little you can do about, really. And it's certainly allowed.

ANDY: I think Rich's point is emotions like fear, regret, confusion, self-pity—boys are brought up to see those as signs of weakness. It's like behaviorally modified out of us from a very young age.

REBECCA: You forgot empathy.

ANDY: *(Directly to Rebecca)* Give me a break. *(To the others)* But it's not just the way men are raised. It's how women are raised to *think* about men. Women say they want more "emotionally available" men, men who share their feelings—

SAM: And we do. What's wrong with that?

ANDY: Nothing's wrong with that, but if that's the case, why can't guys like Mike Dubinsky have a long-term relationship? *(To Rich)* Or your friend from work—the guy who took my ticket for the concert the other night?

RICH: Evan. Evan Sanders.

ANDY: *(Moving toward the sofa)* Why can't these guys find lasting relationships? Mike's a great guy. We can all agree on that, can't we? How many times have we marveled at why women— women we know and have introduced to him—why don't women respond to him? The nicest guy you'll ever meet?

SAM: I think he comes on a little needy, to be honest. A little too eager for a relationship.

REBECCA: I agree. He breaks my heart because he is so damn nice. And thoughtful, and caring. But he probably comes on a little too strong for some women.

ANDY: The guy tears up watching insurance commercials.

RICH: He's always been that way.

SAM: I think it's more about the women he's dated than him. He doesn't make great choices.

ANDY: To some extent, but I really think it's because Mike is truly that "sensitive" Mr. Nice Guy that women—

RICH: *Some* women.

ANDY: *Claim* to be looking for, but when confronted by it, he's suddenly "too needy," "he comes on too strong."

REBECCA: What are you getting at? That women want emotionally distant men who treat them kinda shitty?

RICH: They don't?

ANDY: My point is this: the same way men are brought up to be emotional cripples, women are trained to perpetuate it and reinforce it.

SAM: Ha! Emotional cripple's a little dramatic, Andy.

REBECCA: A little?

ANDY: O.K. O.K. Hobbled? An emotional limp? It's the only way women understand men to be. It's what they've been taught to expect.

SAM: Andy, I think it boils down to the whole communication issue. I understand the way society trains men. I just want the men in my life—

RICH: Excuse me. Men?

*He heads to the kitchen.*

SAM: Certainly the man I'm married to. I want him to be as emotionally trusting and open as he can be. To at least make the effort. And to be as direct and honest in—

ANDY: I don't believe most women want men to be so direct and honest.

REBECCA: *(Annoyed)* What are you talking about? That's the most important thing—

ANDY: B-S. Here's an example: when we're getting ready to go out somewhere, you ask me things like "Does this look alright?" or "Does this make my butt look too big?" You want me to give you a particular answer. You don't want my honest opinion.

SAM: Oh come on, Andy.

ANDY: O.K. Here's an example that's a little less superficial. *(To Rebecca)* A year or so after David was born you went through those few months of hating your job, wanting to find a new job, generally moping around and feeling sorry for yourself. Remember? Not a very pleasant time. And when I finally told you what I honestly thought about it, and about what you should do, you were furious at me. For a good two weeks. If not more.

REBECCA: *(Angrily)* That's because you weren't being very

supportive when I needed you to be supportive.

ANDY: Not true. I was *very* supportive...for the first two months. Painfully supportive. But you didn't want my honest opinion. You just wanted me to continue commiserating about how unfair it all was, about how you were trapped in this insurmountable situation that you weren't doing even one damn thing to extricate yourself from. It wasn't a very pleasant time, Rebecca. And after you asked me for like the thousandth time what I thought, I finally gave you my honest opinion and you got pissed.

*Awkward silence. SAM diverts her eyes. ANDY and REBECCA stare at each other.*

REBECCA: *(Starting slowly)* Well, I'd be lying if I didn't say that I sure did learn a lot about my marriage then.

ANDY: *(Angrily)* So did I, Rebecca. So did I. But don't sit here and claim you want honest and direct communication between us when...when it really matters, you get mad at me for being honest with you.

REBECCA: *(Deflecting)* Can we just agree to try and bring up our son to be honest in a little less...aggressive way?

ANDY: *(Seething)* Sure. How about a little less passive-aggressive, too?

*A longer, more awkward silence. SAM gets up and heads for the table to help clean up dishes. RICH enters from kitchen.*

RICH: Speaking of David—kinda—how's the little guy doing? *(Pause)* Honestly?

*REBECCA, SAM, and RICH laugh nervously, relieving the tension.*

REBECCA: He's fine. Now that he's got the walking thing down, it's a whole new world.

ANDY: *(Grudgingly)* It's mostly running. As if he's got such a busy schedule. He dashes from place to place. Coffee table—oh, gotta get over to that TV right now. Oops. I'm late for pulling all the books off the shelf—better get right over there.

REBECCA: He's slowly working through Andy's entire CD collection.

ANDY: I figure in a few months every one of my CDs will either have a cracked jewel case or a broken hinge.

RICH: I've got a few of those from the last time he was here.

ANDY: Speaking of music—how was the concert the other night?

RICH: Awesome show. It was really good. Probably the best since we saw them in Milwaukee that time.

ANDY: I'm so pissed I couldn't make it. The review in the paper raved about it.

RICH: Yeah. It was great.

ANDY: I bet your brother was in heaven.

RICH: If Chris says they rocked, you know it was good. He's seen them like 20 times.

SAM: I wish I would've been in town for it. I haven't seen them in three years? Four? I asked Rich to pick me up a t-shirt but he blew it off.

*REBECCA stands, going to the dining table to help SAM.*

REBECCA: After I *ruined* Andy's life by having to go out of town that night—

SAM: I don't know how you could face yourself in the mirror.

REBECCA: I still can't. But Andy considered bringing David to the show.

RICH: You'd have shredded the kid's eardrums.

ANDY: I'd just spackle his ears shut.

RICH: I wonder how old a kid would need to be to bring them to a concert.

SAM: *(To Andy)* You weren't really thinking of bringing David to that show, were you?

ANDY: No, I wasn't.

REBECCA: That was the first thing you said when I told you I had to go to Boston. "I know—I'll just bring David along."

ANDY: That was more of a desperate joke. It was denial. I was in the initial stages of denial because I couldn't *believe* you were telling me you had to go to Boston the day before the concert.

REBECCA: I had no choice.

SAM: No babysitter?

ANDY: Not that short notice. You guys are our go-to last-minute bailout. You were still out of town, and I knew damn well where Rich was going to be.

REBECCA: It's not like I planned it, Andy. It came up that day. I had to go.

ANDY: Am I saying anything about it?

REBECCA: It's more the tone.

ANDY: I don't want to get into it, Rebecca. It sucked, but that's what happens sometimes. I'll see them next time they're in town. I'll line-up a babysitter in advance.

REBECCA: *(Looking at her watch)* Speaking of which, we should probably get going. It's getting late.

ANDY: *(Snidely)* And we were just starting to have fun.

RICH: *(Checking his watch)* It's barely 11.

REBECCA: I know, but we have to have the sitter home by midnight.

*ANDY heads toward the closet to gather their coats.*

ANDY: It's one of the joys of parenthood—asleep in bed early on a Saturday night.

RICH: That's one of the joys?

ANDY: Something has to be...

*Fade to black.*

## SCENE THREE

*RICH and SAMANTHA's apartment. Lights on, music playing a little loud. There is a knock on the door. No response. Louder knocking on the door.*

CHRIS: *(From outside)* Open up in there! Music police!

RICH: *(From offstage)* Be right there!

CHRIS: *(From offstage)* Pinch it off bro. The cops are here— they're very annoyed with this musical selection.

*RICH appears from the hallway, zipping up and buckling his belt.*

RICH: Alright already, alright.

*RICH opens door. CHRIS is leaning on doorframe.*

CHRIS: Loafin'?

RICH: I wish. That seafood goes right through me.

*CHRIS enters, closing the door behind him. He's a few years older than RICH. He's dressed casually, notably wearing sunglasses and Chuck Taylor hi-tops. There's a t-shirt over his shoulder.*

CHRIS: Whoa, dude. Light a flare or something. I don't know how Sam lives with you.

RICH: *(Turning music down)* What's up?

CHRIS: Nothing much. I'm heading over to the bar to meet someone Casey at work is trying to set me up with. Thought I'd take a short detour and see what's up with you.

RICH: Not a lot. I thought you took some new woman to the concert with you. Angie?

CHRIS: I did. An*JEL*ica. Total dud. Oh yeah. Here.

*He tosses a t-shirt to RICH.*

RICH: Total dud? That's serious. *(Looking at t-shirt)* What's this?

CHRIS: A t-shirt. A concert t-shirt from the show you blew off.

RICH: You don't want it?

CHRIS: I've got one. I bought that for my dud date. She left it at my house.

RICH: Must not have been too much of a dud date.

CHRIS: Totally one-sided. She was all over me like a bad suit.

RICH: Too bad for you.

CHRIS: It was, 'cause I really wasn't interested, yet the total sleazeball in me wanted to take advantage of the situation. She was a dud, but she was a very foxy dud.

RICH: And?

CHRIS: And what? And nothing. I told her I wasn't interested in pursuing things any further.

RICH: Harsh, dude.

CHRIS: What was I gonna do? Sleep with her? Then spend a few weeks pretending I was interested and "suddenly" realize I wasn't? When I knew I already wasn't?

RICH: So why'd you take her to the show?

CHRIS: I don't know. It was stupid. *(Heading toward kitchen)* You have any decent beer?

RICH. Snob. I think there's something in there from the last time you were here.

CHRIS: *(From kitchen)* It was one of those "last chance" kind of things. Which is why it was stupid from the start. *(Enters from kitchen)* We'd been on like three official dates, and I pretty much knew it was going nowhere, but I figured why not take her to a really cool show—one of my favorite bands—and make sure I wasn't being too hasty.

RICH: And she failed.

CHRIS: No, she didn't fail. It was more like...yeah. She pretty much failed. If you want to look at it that way. Like I said, it was stupid. I should've broken up with her before.

RICH: Did she like the show?

CHRIS: Hard to tell. She was talking my fucking ear off for most of it.

RICH: Ah. That's the death knell right there. She didn't stand a chance.

CHRIS: I finally had to re-direct her to your friend from work. Everet?

RICH: Evan. He's a chatterbox himself.

CHRIS: No shit. They were jawboning all the way through the rest of the show, at the bar afterward, right up until Evan got in a cab to go home. I'm surprised he hasn't asked you for her number.

RICH: I'll let him know you two aren't dating.

CHRIS: The talking was just the topper. She really wasn't my type.

RICH: Anyone who jabbers away at a concert is not your type.

CHRIS: I can usually ignore it when it's just people around me, but when someone you're with is dampening your ear through every song—

RICH: A spitter, too?

CHRIS: She was a bit of a spitter. One of those people who always seem to be sloshing around a mouthful of saliva. Like that teacher at Lincoln School–

RICH: Mrs. Olmsted. I used to bring one of dad's golf towels to class. I sat in the front row.

CHRIS: I sat in the last row and I still got hit.

RICH: Despite the spitting, she was a pretty nice teacher as I recall. I wonder what ever happened to her?

CHRIS: Who knows. The question is, what the hell happened to you?

RICH: What do you mean?

CHRIS: The concert you ditched out on?

RICH: Didn't you get my email?

CHRIS: Yeah, I got it. But I don't buy it.

RICH: Chris, I felt like shit. I came home to take a nap before the show, and when I woke up it was like 10:30. And I still felt like shit. You know I wouldn't have missed that show—

CHRIS: I know. That's why I don't buy it. What? Getting soft in your advanced age?

RICH: No. I was getting dehydrated.

CHRIS: You were horking?

RICH: Almost. It was mostly the other end.

CHRIS: *(Assuming a he-man voice)* I remember a day when you would have thrown on a pair of Depends, duct taped the waist and leg holes closed, and been at the front of that stage sweatin' and stinkin' the joint out.

RICH: *(Laughing)* Don't even rub it in, man. I was really bummed that I missed that show.

CHRIS: Was it something you ate at the coffee shop?

RICH: What coffee shop?

CHRIS: Near your office. Gourmond. The place with the great muffins. When your friend Evan met us at the bar before the show, he said he saw you at Gourmond getting some coffee after work.

RICH: No, no, I didn't eat anything there. I was just picking up my coffee beans I think. I'm pretty sure it was the Mexican food I ate the night before at El Tio. Some baked fish thing with jalapenos. It was really good, actually.

CHRIS: I thought maybe you blew us off for some chick.

RICH: *(Stunned)* What? What are you talking about?

CHRIS: Evan said that when he stopped in at Gourmond that he saw you having coffee with some woman.

RICH: Who knows? I could've been talking to someone there. A lot of people who work in the neighborhood go in there. It could have been anybody. But it wasn't for long—I was already well into the sweating and the need to be within 20 feet of a bathroom at that point.

CHRIS: I told Evan while we were at the show that you were either dead or in the hospital. No other possible reasons you'd miss it.

RICH: I had a fever, dude. I must've been on the crapper a dozen times that night.

CHRIS: The cans at the club are real clean, too.

RICH: It would've been a nightmare.

CHRIS: There's probably a bootleg of the show already available on some fan site.

RICH: There is. Andy sent me a link earlier this week.

CHRIS: Man, was he pissed when Rebecca had to go out of town.

RICH: I think it's still a sensitive spot. They were here for dinner a few days after the show. Seemed to be a touchy subject between them

CHRIS: Isn't most everything a touchy subject between them?

RICH: Seems that way. Especially in the past couple of years.

CHRIS: It's like hanging out with the Bickersons when they're together.

RICH: I much prefer them individually in a social situation.

CHRIS: You see them more than I do now. But before they had David, they were out a lot. And there always seemed to be some tit-for-tat, bickery thing going between them.

RICH: They're two really opinionated, really strong-willed people. I think it was part of the whole attraction.

CHRIS: But it seems to have turned on itself, you know? Andy is such a heel-digger-inner. He was like that when he was a kid, remember?

RICH: Hell yeah. If he didn't want to do something, there was no way in hell you were going to convince him. His way or the highway. It really used to piss me off.

CHRIS: I know it did. It used to piss me off that you'd let him call the shots so much.

RICH: He was always kind of the de facto leader of our pack because he's almost two years older than me. I always figured he was such a tyrant because the older kids like you and Alex and Stevie and all those guys would blow him off.

CHRIS: *(At the window)* Hey—those boats out on the lake reminded me: have you talked to dad lately?

RICH: A couple of weeks ago. Why?

CHRIS: He and Alice are going down to the Florida Keys on some boating excursion.

RICH: Dad doesn't boat. He hates boats.

CHRIS: I know. But Alice does. She has some friends down there who have a big boat. They're going on a three or four day trip. Gonna do some deep-sea fishing dad said.

RICH: Dad hates fishing.

CHRIS: *(Laughing)* I know. I reminded him of how much he liked it when we forced him to take us as kids. *(Imitating their father)* "Sitting around baking in the sun trying to concentrate on a thin little line in the water..."

RICH: Fishing on a boat? Does he realize how much sunscreen he's going to have to wear?

CHRIS: That is so funny you said that—I blew him shit about the very same thing.

RICH: He hates the feeling of it on his skin. He never wears it. And he always ends up with a sunburn. He's going to roast on that boat.

CHRIS: He says Alice will take care of him. And she probably will. He kinda just goes along with what she says sometimes.

RICH: I know. I've seen it happen.

CHRIS: I asked him what he was going to do on like the second day when he's sitting there on the deck, staring at a bobber in the Gulf, sweating like a horse, listening to his shoulders sizzle, and realizing that all he wants to do is get the hell off the boat and into some air conditioning.

RICH: What did he say?

CHRIS: Swim! *(They laugh)* Sharks and all.

RICH: I'll have to give him a call. Find out what the hell he's thinking.

CHRIS: Be warned though: Alice's daughter either just had a baby or is just about to have one, so he may be on the grandkid tip with you.

RICH: But not with you, of course.

CHRIS: He sure is, but he knows his odds are better with you and Sam right now.

RICH: I know, I know. It comes up from time to time. More with dad than with mom.

CHRIS: I don't think mom's ever asked me about kids. Not even when I was married.

RICH: She wasn't thrilled with the idea of being a grandmother that young. Or with you being a parent that young, either.

CHRIS: That would've been the dumbest thing I could've done at the time. Second dumbest—getting married that young was the dumbest.

RICH: I couldn't even imagine it. I got married at 32 and I still wondered if I was ready for it.

CHRIS: There's a huge difference between 32 and 22. At least at 32 you've lived on your own for a while, had a real job or two, maybe bought a car, maybe smashed your car in a grocery store parking lot—

RICH: Alright now.

CHRIS: But you know what I mean? At 32 you at least have a little bit of a clue and at least a reasonable idea about responsibility. And how difficult relationships can be. At 22, you don't know shit. You know how to party alright. You still have no real idea how to fuck—but you're an expert at fuckin' up. You think you know a lot of shit, but all you have is a college degree and some cash and a dangerously high opinion of yourself.

*We hear keys jingling outside the door. RICH crosses and opens the door. It's SAM.*

RICH: Hey babe.

*SAM enters, carrying a grocery bag, briefcase and purse. She kisses RICH excitedly.*

SAM: I think I've got some news. *(She sees CHRIS and halts.)* What are you doing here?

CHRIS: There's a warm welcome. Nice to see you too, Sam.

SAM: I didn't mean it that way. *(Meeting CHRIS for a hug)* Sorry about that. Are you two going out tonight or something?

CHRIS: Let me help you.

*He reaches for the grocery bag.*

SAM: *(Abruptly)* No. I've got it.

*She beelines to the kitchen.*

RICH: Chris just stopped by on his way to blind date #247.

CHRIS: I was led to believe she was fully sighted. Slight limp and bad hearing, but full ocular functionality.

*SAM is in the kitchen. We hear her rustling through the grocery bag, items dropping on the table or floor.*

RICH: Hysterical. Are you working stand-up? *(Crosses to kitchen)* Need another beer?

SAM: *(Quickly, from the kitchen)* I'll get them.

*We hear a cabinet slam shut. Then the refrigerator door opens and closes.*

CHRIS: No thanks for me. I gotta get going.

*RICH meets SAM at the kitchen door; takes beer.*

RICH: None for you?

SAM: No – my stomach's been a little funky all day.

CHRIS: You didn't eat any Mexican fish "things" for dinner last night, did you?

SAM: No. Why?

CHRIS: Those are the "things" that had Rich tied to the can the night of—

RICH: *(Abruptly)* C'mon, Chris. Do we have to talk about my bowels again? This is nothing new to Sam. It's the burden she bears in this marriage. Do we need to keep reminding her?

SAM: *(Looking at RICH, then at CHRIS)* O.K. How long have you two been drinking here?

CHRIS: Since noon. Never open a bottle before noon.

RICH: Greenwich meantime, of course.

SAM: Of course. You're professionals. *(To CHRIS)* So another blind date, Chris?

CHRIS: More of an arranged meeting. My friend Casey at work wants me to meet a friend of hers. You know the drill.

SAM: What happened to that woman you were just starting to date. Angie?

CHRIS: An*JEL*ica. It wasn't working out.

RICH: *(Crossing to kitchen)* She was a spitter and a show-talker.

SAM: Cross her right off the list no doubt.

CHRIS: As I told Richard—hey, didn't we used to call you Dick when you were a kid?—it was more than just the spitting and talking.

SAM: You broke up with her I take it?

CHRIS: Why drag it out. She wasn't really even my type.

SAM: This is becoming something of a pattern for you lately, Chris.

CHRIS: I know, but I figure at this point, I'm 39 years old; I don't really have that much time or patience for the extended mix dating ritual. After a few dates, you know whether or not the thing has legs.

SAM: I seem to recall you dated something without legs a few years ago.

CHRIS: Touché.

RICH: *(Entering from kitchen)* It was many months of dating before I knew this relationship with Sam really had any potential.

CHRIS: But early on you knew you wanted to keep dating her, right?

SAM: I knew I did. Right away. Didn't know I'd end up marrying the guy...

CHRIS: Not with that gastric affliction.

SAM: So when do you have to meet this new, *new* woman?

CHRIS: *(Checking watch)* Seven thirty. 'Bout 15 minutes. I should get going actually.

RICH: Hey - what was your news, Sam?

SAM: Oh, just work news. About a trip to Japan this fall.

CHRIS: Great country. Tokyo is like an amusement park.

RICH: Can spouses go?

SAM: Don't know yet.

RICH: Well that totally dwarfs my big news.

SAM: What news?

*RICH holds up his left hand to show SAM his wedding ring.*

RICH: The guy finally got my ring sized correctly.

SAM: Finally. It only took him a month.

RICH: The third time was the charm.

CHRIS: Getting a little puffy in the hands, huh?

SAM: *(Suddenly to CHRIS)* Where are you meeting this woman?

CHRIS: At the Gingerman.

SAM: Let me guess: El Tio for dinner?

CHRIS: Sushi. She says it's her favorite.

SAM: That's promising.

CHRIS: *(Swallowing the last of his beer)* We'll see. Enough yappin'. Off to meet another potential dud date.

SAM: C'mon Chris. You've got to go in with a little more positive attitude than that.

RICH: Yeah. She could be Ms. Right.

CHRIS: She could be Ms. Very Wrong, too.

SAM: *(Hugging CHRIS)* Well good luck either way.

CHRIS: Thanks. *(To RICH)* I'll call or email you about next weekend.

RICH: Sounds good. See ya Chris.

*CHRIS exits. SAM goes directly to the kitchen.*

RICH: So Tokyo sounds cool.

SAM: *(From kitchen)* There is no Tokyo trip.

RICH: What do you mean there's no Tokyo trip? I thought you said you had some big news?

*SAM enters from the kitchen with a box behind her back.*

SAM: Uh-uh.

*She shows RICH the box.*

RICH: *(Reading box, then)* NO WAY!

SAM: Yes way! I'm almost sure. I'm over two weeks late. Almost three. And I'm never late.

RICH: *(Now stunned)* Oh my god.

SAM: Aren't you excited?

RICH: I'm...I'm...stunned.

SAM: *(Hugging RICH)* I'm stunned too, but I've had a couple of weeks to think about it.

RICH: How come you didn't say anything?

SAM: I didn't want to jinx it. You know how superstitious I am. *(Pause)* You do remember that we've been trying to do this, right?

RICH: Yes, yes. Of course. *(Hugging SAM)* Of course I do. It's just...it's one thing to talk about it, think about it. But now that it seems more real...

SAM: It's too weird. I know. I've been carrying this secret around and it's too weird.

RICH: After trying for so long.

SAM: *(Opening box, pulling out directions)* All that trying wasn't such a bad thing.

RICH: No, no. Of course not. I just kind of assumed the usual monthly flow happened when you were on your trip. I even saw you pack the tampons.

SAM: *(Distractedly, reading the directions)* I was already a little late. I was expecting it to happen, but it didn't.

RICH: *(Sitting on the couch)* Wow. That's all I can say. Wow.

SAM: *(Sitting next to him)* I couldn't believe I was buying this at the store. I hid it at the bottom of the cart in case I ran into someone we know.

RICH: *(Suddenly)* I'm gonna be a dad? You're gonna be a mom? I can't deal with it. We're gonna be someone's parents?

SAM: I know. We're going to be great parents.

RICH: *(Looking at the test stick)* So what's the deal? We just pee on this?

SAM: *I* pee on it. Simple as that. Then we wait... *(checking instructions)* three minutes and check to see if a pink line appears in that little window.

RICH: Does it say if there has to be a certain amount of pee that hits this thing?

SAM: You want to get a measuring cup? No—just need to get it wet.

RICH: So this is what the people in the commercials for these things are talking about? Peeing on a little plastic stick? And it tells you if you're going to be a parent.

SAM: Exactly. Let's find out.

*They both head toward the bathroom. SAM stops RICH.*

SAM: I can handle it from here.

RICH: Oh yeah. Sorry.

*SAM exits to the bathroom but immediately returns to RICH, taking the test from him.*

SAM: I'll need the pee stick.

RICH: That would help. *(As bathroom door closes)* Sam!

SAM: *(From bathroom)* Yes?

RICH: Just pee on it and close the little slider. No fair looking first.

SAM: O.K.

*As he waits, RICH paces, occasionally gesturing in excitement. The toilet flushes. Door opens. SAM enters from the bathroom.*

SAM: We'll know soon. And I didn't peek.

RICH: *(Hugging SAM)* Well even if it doesn't turn out positive, this was good practice for the shock of the whole thing.

SAM: I'm pretty sure, Rich. Did you check your watch?

RICH: *(Looking at watch)* I didn't. O.K. So, like, two-and-a-half minutes.

SAM: It already seems like ten.

RICH: So the deal is there has to be a pink line in that little window.

SAM: Correct. *(Checking directions)* It doesn't matter how dark the line is. Any line means you're pregnant.

RICH: *(Checks his watch. Pause)* I still can't believe it.

SAM: It's what we wanted, right?

RICH: Yes. It is. I'm like a jumbled mix of excited, stunned, freaked, worried, scared...

SAM: Me too. Or I was at first. Now it's basically a steady mix of excited and scared. How much time?

RICH: *(Checking watch)* About a minute and a half. So let's try to figure it out. The due date would be what? Late November?

SAM: I think so. Somewhere around there. I remember Rebecca telling me once that doctors use this wheel thingy that's based on your last period.

RICH: You didn't tell her, did you?

SAM: No. It was when they were having David she told me that. I haven't told anyone.

RICH: O.K. *(Checks watch)* It'll be fall. Starting to get cold.

SAM: Which isn't so bad. At least I won't be eight months pregnant in August and big as a house. I'd be a sweaty mess.

RICH: We'll need to do something about the draft from this window here. Which bedroom will he have? The office? Or ours?

SAM· We'll figure it out—we'll have the next seven or eight months to worry about it.

RICH: Names! We'll have to decide on names! We both like Patrick for a boy, right?

SAM: I like Patrick. I like Jack, too.

RICH: Jack's O.K. "Jack Flaherty." "Patrick Flaherty." Hey—whose last name?

SAM: I don't know. I'm not big on the hyphenated names.

RICH: Neither am I.

SAM: What's the time?

RICH: *(Looks at watch)* Maybe baby time?

SAM: Let's see.

*They rush to the bathroom. Pause. They return to the living room, looking slightly dazed. RICH holds the test.*

RICH: That's pink alright.

SAM: Bright as can be.

RICH: We're going to have a baby, Sam.

SAM: Actually, I'm going to have a baby. But I can't think of a better guy to have it with. Or a better dad.

RICH: Or a better mom. *(Pause. Then quietly)* Wow.

SAM: You said it. *(Looks at RICH)* Are you O.K.?

RICH: *(Muffled)* Yeah. Just stunned again.

SAM: Rich, are you crying?

*RICH lifts his head slowly to look at SAM, tears on his cheeks. He shakes his head 'no.'*

SAM: Oh baby.

*She hugs him. Fade to black.*

## SCENE FOUR

*RICH's office. Small, windowless, spare. There is a TV monitor and video/stereo equipment, with plenty of tape and discs stacked in various places. He is pacing around his desk wearing a telephone headset.*

RICH: See how simple and clean that looks? One compelling image of a professional looking woman at a moment of some undetermined crisis. And just that one line at the bottom of the ad: "Isn't it time you decide what kind of day you'll have?" Product name lower right. *(Pause)* Obviously—you're not a pharmaceutical company. *(Pause)* I have no idea what Xyntella is, Marvin. From my perspective, I don't care. It's the effectiveness of the ad I want you to look at. It gets your attention. It makes you wonder what's going on in the picture. And how can this Xyntella let you decide your day?

*Pause, listening. RICH rolls his eyes and sits in his desk chair. He begins typing at his computer.*

Here—I'm pulling it up on line. Looks like a depression drug. Like Prozac. But what I like about the ad is the way it pulls you in, engages you. That's the style of ad campaign I think you should go with. Something that will make people see themselves in it and say, "Yeah, that's me, too."

*Pause. He gestures in frustration.*

Marvin, I know. I know you're not a pharmaceutical company. Trust me—I am fully aware that you sell cookies. How about this— *(Phone beeps)* Can I put you on hold for a second Marvin? Thanks. *(Switches lines)* Hello, this is Rich. *(Pause)* Andy. What up? *(Pause)* Me? I'm in hell. Absolute hell. Turner asked me to personally handle this new account— family-owned cookie maker from Milwaukee is going national. Turner has some connection with the family. But the "marketing" guy I'm dealing with is 2700 years old and is thinking neighborhood circular while I'm trying to get him to understand the importance of branding. Actually, I should go— *(Pause)* You're asking me if I want to consume a hop-based beverage with you after work? Yeah, that should be fine. Anything up? *(Pause)* No reason. But the last time you wanted to grab a beer after work and talk was when you told me you and Rebecca were having a baby. *(Pause)* O.K. See you then. Bye. *(Switches lines again)* Marvin? Marvin? Sorry about that. It's one of those days around here. This is what I was going to suggest: picture a series of ads—print ads, in newspapers and magazines, as well as online—where we have a variety of men and women, girls and boys, in various poses sneaking one of your cookies. Take a humorous approach. Like a shot of an older executive type at a board meeting with the big long table behind him and he's swiveled his high-back chair around and is eating a cookie with a sneaky, guilty look on his face. The tag would be something like "When you need one, you simply need one." Or "You can't fight the urge. Why even try?" With Uncle Dave's Cookies in big letters at the bottom of the ad.

*Pause. He shakes his head, exasperated, and begins pacing his office again.*

You're right, Marvin. What was I thinking? I should never have even mentioned the pharmaceutical ad—way off there, you're right. But you get the idea of what I'm thinking about? *(Pause)* Exactly. Humor sells big. Some of the most effective and famous ad campaigns have been funny. People remember them. And if the plan is to move into TV, you're already establishing a visual— *(Pause)* Excuse me? *(Pause)* Um…well, because normally it would be rude for a big executive to eat a cookie during an important meeting. That's why he's sneaking it with his back turned to the table. The cookies are so good that— *(Pause)* Exactly. He's just gotta have one right there. *(Pause)* At the board meeting. *(Pause)* With his back turned—so no one will see him. *(Pause)* Or want one—that's true. He might not want to share. *(Pause)* Exactly. That's why it's kind of a funny ad.

*The intercom buzzes.*

No, that was my intercom. They'll have to wait. *(Pause)* Well, there'd be a series of these kinds of ads. We could have a woman making a speech duck down below the podium to sneak a cookie.

A little boy on a pitcher's mound with his glove in front of his face could be eating a cookie— *(Pause)* Well, you'd shoot the picture from the side so you could see the boy eating the cookie.

*The intercom buzzes again.*

Mine again, Marvin. But do you see how a print campaign like this can build excitement about your product? People who see these ads will wonder "Are they that good? I've got to try some." *(Pause)* *I* know they're that good, Marvin. I've got a box of them here in my office. I've been snacking on them all day. The point is to make consumers curious about them so they'll go out and buy Uncle Dave's Cookies. And this kind of ad campaign is how you begin to build brand recognition. *(Pause)* Yes, but we're talking about people outside of the Milwaukee area.

*The office door opens. CASSANDRA enters and closes the door behind her. RICH is stunned. He smiles briefly, then returns to his office chair, sitting gingerly and watching CASSANDRA the whole time. She drops her backpack next to a chair across from where RICH sits, staring back at him.*

RICH: *(Startled, back to the phone call)* Yes, yes I heard you Marvin. I'm actually due in a meeting about five minutes ago. Let me call you back tomorrow.

*Pause. He turns away from CASSANDRA and casually removes his wedding ring.*

O.K. That's fine. Why don't you call me tomorrow when you have some time to talk? *(Pause)* Oh sure. 3-1-2-4-6-7-3-9-0-0. That's the general line—they'll be able to put you through. *(Pause. He forces a laugh.)* That's right—so good you have to sneak them. O.K. Good talking to you Marvin. O.K. O.K. Goodbye.

*RICH disconnects the line and takes off his headset. He tries a smile.*

RICH: Some of these clients don't quite—

CASS: Did you give him the right number?

*Pause. CASSANDRA leans closer to his desk.*

CASS: Maybe if I was a client you would've given me your actual phone number.

RICH: What are you talking about?

CASS: *(Flipping a piece of paper on his desk)* This. It's your own handwriting.

RICH: It is. I jumbled these two numbers. Probably mixed it up with my work number.

CASS: Don't give me that bullshit. At least have the cajones to admit it. Don't be a weasel about it.

*Pause. RICH looks down at the floor and slides his wedding ring into a pocket.*

RICH: I'm sorry, Cassandra.

CASS: So am I. You seemed very nice. I liked you.

*Pause.*

RICH: Uh...how have you been?

CASS: Fine. But you would've known that had you picked up the phone and called me. I did give you my phone number.

RICH: I know. And I'm sorry. It's just that...well, when Samantha came back—

CASS: Who's Samantha?

RICH: *(Genuinely confused)* The woman I live with. My ex...ex.

CASS: Oh. Samantha. Silly me. I thought you lived with a woman named Sally. Sal, I believe you called her.

RICH: *(Pause. Then quietly)* Her name's Samantha. When she came back from her trip, we had a long series of talks over the next few days and kind of came to an understanding about things.

CASS: Came to understand that you couldn't possibly live without each other, I presume?

RICH: Something like that.

CASS: Of course! Isn't that predictable.

RICH: It's true.

CASS: "Something like that?" How would Sal or Sam or whatever her real name is feel if she heard your strong commitment there? "Something like that."

RICH: We realized we wanted to be together. Is that better?

CASS: At least have the conviction of your actions. Of your feelings.

RICH: I do. That's how we feel about it. How I feel about it. That's why I didn't call.

CASS: Well I did try to call you. But I had a number that wasn't in service. And that's what made me mad.

RICH: I wasn't sure if—

CASS: I know why you did it. That's what infuriates me. I would much rather you have given me your correct number and then tell me you weren't interested. Or have just not bothered going through the motions of giving me this phony number and told me you didn't think you wanted to pursue things any further. It would have hurt, but that I can handle. This lying bullshit...you American men are so...

*Pause. CASSANDRA shakes her head and smiles.*

RICH: So what?

CASS: So what—precisely.

*Pause.*

CASS: Look, Rich. I'm not here to be some spurned, *Fatal Distraction*-type crazy woman—

RICH: *(Quietly) Attraction.* The movie was *Fatal Attraction.*

CASS: *Attraction*—whatever it was. I'm not going to kill your pets or show up in your bathtub. I understand you and your girlfriend are back together. That's fine. But I abhor cowardice, Rich. And if me showing up here at your office gave you even a few minutes of genuine concern about the way you behaved, then I'm glad. *(Slowly leans over his desk)* Have respect for women, Rich. At least this woman.

*She turns and picks up her bag.*

RICH: Cassandra?

CASS: Yes.

RICH: Please accept my apology. I acted poorly.

CASS: Rudely.

RICH: That too.

CASS: And selfishly.

RICH: O.K. I'll give you that. But I—

CASS: Don't forget cowardly.

RICH: How could I? What I'm trying to say is—

CASS: Don't say anything. Don't say anything.

RICH: O.K.

CASS: I'd offer to buy you a cup of coffee across the street, as a kind of closure to this whole…tryst, if you will, but that's how all this trouble began. So I'll say buena suerte to you Rich, and take my leave.

*She shakes his hand, kisses him on the cheek, and exits. RICH stands at his desk, staring at the door. His hand touches his cheek for a moment. He slowly sits in his chair, slips on his headset, and dials the phone. He pulls his wedding ring from his pocket.*

RICH: Hello Sam? How's your day going…?

*Fade to black.*

## SCENE FIVE

*RICH and ANDY are seated at a bar. They are in their work
clothes.*

ANDY: Remember when we were at your place for dinner?

RICH: Yeah.

ANDY: Well, that dinner conversation sort of sparked a huge
fight.

RICH: Really?

ANDY: Yes. Really. Lasted a few days. It was all the things that
piss us off that the other does, the way we're raising David, the
issues we have with each other's families. Actually, the issues
Rebecca has with *my* mother. All of it. Nine years of the petty
shit, the big issues, the in-between stuff—

RICH: Sounds exhausting.

ANDY: It was. And it got nasty. Both of us got nasty.

RICH: Sometimes that kind of big purge can actually be helpful—
to get at the underlying root of the problems.

ANDY: We've always done this kind of purging from time to time,
but not so much since we had David. There's just not all that
much time to focus on the relationship with the kid around. You'll
see what I mean.

RICH: And you both can be a little volatile at times.

ANDY: Master of understatement. But after we'd both sort of
settled down, calmed down enough to discuss rather than indict,
we started weeding out the important stuff from the unimportant
bullshit.

RICH: How'd that go?

ANDY: Pretty good. Though we still see the essential problems as being different.

RICH: And those are?

ANDY: Those are that I think Rebecca has become much less interested in us as a couple ever since David came along. And I don't mean the basic distraction of having a kid around. I'm talking about a general disinterest in what I'm doing, what we as a couple are going through. To her it's immaterial. It's all about the boy now.

RICH: And her take on it?

ANDY: I'm not done with my take yet. That's one; two is this fucked up "should" thing. She's always worried about what we *should* be doing rather than what we *are* doing. It's as if there's some model couple, some ideal mom-dad thing she wants to be that I don't have any interest in. Like this religion thing. I haven't had any interest in church or religion since I was like 13. But she's got this real bug about us going to church now. Us as a family. She's more than welcome to go herself, take David along if she wants, but for her it's important that we all go. To me, that's a big issue. Religion's a big deal—and if I don't believe, I'm not going to go through the motions to appease Rebecca. Or to make sure David sees his mom and dad going to church together because it's an important part of our lives. My dad did that shit for years, and he hated it. And I'm simply not going to do it.

RICH: So you're flexible there—that's good to see. Is there a three?

ANDY: Yes. But it's all tied in with one and two. Three is the sex. Or the lack thereof. In the last six months I think we've had sex twice. Maybe one and a half times.

RICH: One and a half? How do you get the half?

ANDY: Trust me—it happens. And perfunctorily at that.

RICH: You know, as empty experiences go, perfunctory sex ain't so bad.

ANDY: I'm not kidding here, Rich.

RICH: I know you're not—just trying to loosen it up a little.

ANDY: You don't have to—this is serious shit to me, you know.

RICH: Sorry, Andy. *(Pause)* So what's Rebecca's take?

ANDY: She feels I'm not interested in us as a couple either. That part we see similarly. I want us to still be a little bit of the people—and the couple—that we were before becoming parents. Going out to dinner, going to concerts and movies and plays. I know we can't do that stuff now like we used to, but I think we still need to try when we can.

RICH: It sounds like you both want to rekindle that couple thing you—

ANDY: We do. But I want to do this "insubstantial" stuff—her word—whereas she wants to be more of an old couple of parents—

RICH: You're words, right?

ANDY: Right. Doing things with other parents, getting involved with the local school organizations, making all this time in our already packed schedules to spend time with David's sitter and her family.

RICH: I gotta say those seem like reasonable activities...

ANDY: *(Pause)* There's nothing wrong with doing that stuff, Rich. I just can't deal with that being the *only* shit we do as a couple. Our free time, our alone together time is practically non-existent, Rich. When we can plan a date and get a babysitter for a Saturday night, I don't want to go to some fucking potluck dinner sponsored by one of the neighborhood organizations. I want to go to a nice restaurant, see a movie, go see a band—something that brings me actual joy. And for wanting that, Rebecca says I've become too selfish. That's her main thing, her #1: that I've become selfish.

*A pause between them. They both sip from their beers.*

RICH: There's got be a balance in there somewhere, Andy. It's just a matter of finding it. Hit or miss maybe.

ANDY: I think what really pisses me off is the "insubstantial" thing. That somehow all the shit we fell in love doing together was just worthless kid stuff. That somehow being parents now we have to become different people. Which I think is complete bullshit. I love David. I love him more than anything or being I've ever known in my entire life. But I am afraid of becoming someone that I am not. Someone that I don't even like. Marriage, then the kid—I've already happily altered my life and my thinking severely. I refuse to lose some of that essential shit that is me. *(Pause)* And I think Rebecca's becoming this "should be" version of some...some imagined model of what a mother should be. *(Pause)* And I don't know how much I really care for that person.

*Another pause between them.*

RICH: So, um, where's it at between you two now?

ANDY: We're going to try some marriage counseling.

RICH: Really?

ANDY: Really. I'm a little hesitant about it because I'm beginning to wonder if these basic rifts between us—the core stuff, the real elemental stuff—I'm worried that they may not be marriage counsel-able.

RICH: You have to go into it with some commitment, Andy. You can't go grudgingly.

ANDY: I'm not. I want it to help. I think it could be a good thing for both of us.

RICH: Can I ask a blunt question?

ANDY: Sure.

RICH: Do you still love Rebecca?

*Long, thoughtful pause. ANDY takes a long drink and slowly turns to his friend.*

ANDY: I don't know. I honestly am not sure who she is now, or who she's becoming. I love the woman I fell in love with. But I'm just not sure if she's still there, or if enough of her is still there.

RICH: Wow. I didn't realize...

ANDY: I don't know if I realized it either until after we had this huge drag-out fight.

RICH: Maybe counseling will help—help you both figure out where you're at. And who you are right now.

ANDY: I'm really hoping it does. But there's more at play here, Rich.

RICH: It sounds like there's a lot at play here—

ANDY: I think Rebecca's been having an affair.

RICH: *(Spit-take)* WHAT!?

ANDY: I think she's been having an affair.

RICH: I heard you, but why?

ANDY: I think it's all part of why she seems to have such little interest in us as a couple.

RICH: I meant why do you suspect that she's been having an affair?

ANDY: A number of things. For the past four months she's been working on this project in Boston.

RICH: Yeah, I know.

ANDY: She's been going to Boston a lot, they've been here in Chicago a lot, and she has been putting in way more time with these people than she has in years at that job.

RICH: But that's nothing to—

ANDY: Wait a second. I said there were a number of reasons. Hear me out on this. So there's all the extra work, all this time in Boston. That's fine—I understand the needs of a job. But when she went to Boston the week we were supposed to see that concert, that was totally last minute. She tells me Tuesday night that she has to go Thursday through Friday. It sucked, really big for me, but again, I had to understand. Important client, she needed to go cover for her boss who'd fucked things up a little bit. Fine. Then Friday evening, while she's flying home, her boss calls the house to ask her something. I tell him she's on her way back from Boston—which he should know, right? The whole premise of her having to go there was to cover his ass. But he doesn't even seem to know she's been in Boston the past two days. "Back there again?" he says. Real surprised sounding. I wanted to unload on the guy. Yeah she's there, covering your ass! But something about his tone...he sounded genuinely surprised.

RICH: But that's nothing to make such a major accusation about.

ANDY: You're right. So I tell her about her boss calling for her at home and she gets all nervous. She tried to pass it off as forgetfulness. But I know Rebecca. Normally she would've blown a gasket over the fact that he sounded surprised. She was pissed she had to go in the first place, right? Or so she said. And then we were at your place for dinner, and you saw how she was. How we were.

RICH: That explains some of the tension, but I really think you're—

ANDY: Wait, Rich, let me finish. So like a week or so after we had this big fight, I have to drive out to the burbs to meet with some new clients. I left my wallet at home—no license, no cash. I have to go by the condo and get it before I drive way the hell out to this client. It's like 1 o'clock in the afternoon, I walk into the apartment, and the shower's running. It's Rebecca. Her work clothes are in a heap outside the shower.

RICH: *(Pause)* What did she say?

ANDY: Nothing. I didn't say anything to her. I wanted to. I wanted to scream "what the fuck is going on here!?" But I didn't. I grabbed my wallet and left.

RICH: That doesn't look so good.

ANDY: *(Becoming increasingly angry)* No. It doesn't. But I didn't even know how to approach it. I was stunned. She works way the hell down in the south Loop—it's not like she could've "been in the area" or any of that bullshit. I was furious. And stunned. I didn't know what to do. Or say. And then that night, while we're making dinner, it comes out that these fuckers from Boston are in town, *again*, and how much of her time they've been taking up, blah-blah-blah. Two days after the shower thing, she has to work late—*again*. She comes home at like 12:30, saying they ordered in dinner and had to get this presentation done for the next day. But it was all bullshit, Rich. It was bullshit.

RICH: How do you know it was all bullshit?

ANDY: Because she never once answered my calls to her office or her cell phone. That's how I know. You know Rebecca, Rich. She answers her cell phone in the fucking movies.

RICH: That one time she answered it in the bathroom—

ANDY: But she smelled different, Rich.

RICH: She what?

ANDY: She smelled different. You know how Sam smells? The scent of her soap, her shampoo, her perfume, her sweat—you know those smells?

RICH: I do.

ANDY: Well I know Rebecca's smell, too. And she didn't smell like her that night. Nothing nasty, mind you. But it was some other smell. Soap or something. Shampoo. It wasn't her, Rich.

*Long pause. Finally, RICH reaches out and puts his hand on ANDY'S arm.*

RICH: I don't know what to say, Andy.

ANDY: Neither do I. Neither do I. It's all I think about, but I have no idea what to say.

RICH: When...when did the smell thing happen?

ANDY: Just last week. And we're supposed to have our first marriage counseling session tomorrow morning. *(Pause)* That should be a fucking blast.

RICH: I'm really sorry to hear this, Andy. I... *(Pause)* What are you going to do?

ANDY: I don't know. I really have no idea. It was all I could do not to explode at her over the weekend. I pretty much found every excuse to not be at home. I even took David out with me on Saturday to get an oil change. Ended up going to see some kids movie for the afternoon.

*ANDY'S cell phone rings. He takes it out of his pocket, looks at it, and puts it on the table.*

ANDY: Rebecca. I need to be back by 7:00. She's driving her mother to some friend's house for dinner. At least I think she is.

I'm really sorry to have dumped all of this on you, Rich. But I really haven't had anyone I could talk to about it.

RICH: It's no problem, Andy. I just wish I had something more to offer.

ANDY: I think I really just needed to say all this to someone else before we go to that counselor.

RICH: Are you going to talk to Rebecca about all this before tomorrow?

ANDY: I don't know. I think I have to. I mean, we're supposed to be going to see this woman tomorrow to start working on saving our marriage, yet I'm pretty sure my wife is having an affair. What the fuck, you know?

RICH: Wow. I don't know what to—

ANDY: I've been wavering the past couple of days between uncontrollable rage at her, at the thought of someone else touching her, of her wanting that and enjoying it, and this really strange sense of worried calm. Like, O.K., if she slept with someone, fine. One time thing. I can deal with it. But what does this mean to the whole thing? Our marriage, our family...it's all so fucking involved. It's such a huge web. It's not like when we were just out of college, going out with women for six months, a year. Breaking up was so easy. Return each other's records and clothes and shit. It was so easy to let that go and move on. But this thing now...there's so much more at stake. *(Pause)* Maybe it's a sign of some small bit of maturity that my anger at Rebecca is subsumed by trying to keep a clear head about what all this could mean to us. As a family.

RICH: True. There's another person to think about other than you.

ANDY: It's been breaking my heart with David. He has no idea what is going on around him. No clue whatsoever.

*ANDY pauses, growing angry and upset.*

ANDY: Man, I never wanted to have a divorced kid. I don't want that, Rich. Remember how we all used to think about Carl Bigglio when we were growing up? His dad would drop him off at home and he always ran right into the house before his dad's car was even off the curb. I never want other kids to think that sad-ass shit about my son. But if Rebecca and I end up getting divorced after all this, that's what will happen. And when he gets older and he learns why we got divorced...what's he going to think of his mom? Or of his dad, who couldn't get beyond a simple affair? This is the shit I'm thinking about Rich.

RICH: It's understandable, Andy. Totally understandable. I'd be thinking the same stuff if I had an affair—if I found out Sam was having an affair. But let's not just jump right to divorce. I think you need to confront Rebecca about this tonight, Andy. Honesty is the key. As calmly as you possibly can, just ask her—

*ANDY'S cell phone rings again. He glances at the caller ID.*

ANDY: FUCK YOU!

RICH: Maybe a little more calmly than that. But get it out on the table.

ANDY: I know, I know. I'm going to. I gotta run. But you know what's gnawing at me probably the most of all?

RICH: What's that?

ANDY: That she brought this shit into our marriage. That's what really pisses me off. We've been having trouble the past year or so, admittedly. Probably obvious to you and Sam. But instead of us figuring out something together, Rebecca went out and brought this bullshit into our marriage. Brought this made-for-TV-movie cliché bullshit into our marriage. That's the thing that may be unforgivable.

RICH: I...I guess you never know. People learn to forgive, Andy. At least after some time has passed.

ANDY: *(Standing, gathering his phone, briefcase, keys.)* I gotta go. Thanks for listening to all this, Rich.

RICH: No problem. I'm always here. Especially if it involves beer and a steamy shower story.

ANDY: I prefer that they don't feature either of our wives. Say hi to Sam.

RICH: Will do.

ANDY: Wish me luck.

RICH: Luck. Let me know how it goes. And Andy: remember, as calmly as you can.

*ANDY exits. RICH sits and watches after him for a moment. He turns back to his beer, runs his hands through his hair, and stares ahead, worried. Fade to black.*

## SCENE SIX

*SAM and RICH'S apartment. They are looking and sorting through a few boxes of baby clothes. Both are still wearing their work clothes.*

SAM: Some of this stuff is really cute. Look at this. *(She holds up an infant jumper)* I think this could work for a boy or girl.

RICH: It's tiny, isn't? It's like doll clothes. Look at these shoes. *(Holds up a pair of infant shoes)* I mean, you could barely fit a small dog's paw into this thing.

SAM: I can't believe how much clothes is in these boxes. When Rebecca said they had a ton of it, she wasn't kidding.

RICH: *(Holding up an infant onesie)* Why even bother having this short sleeve on here? It's like a little flap. I think my favorite thing I've read so far in the expecting book is when they described the beginning of the arm and leg formation as "buds."

SAM: I remember that. Like it's a flower.

RICH: And the picture they showed—you know, the ultrasound-looking picture—was exactly that: little tiny buds. That's what I think I'm going to start calling him. Her. It. "Bud." It's a good nickname.

SAM: Sounds like some old guy regular at a bar: Bud.

RICH: To me it sounds like an old guy playing horseshoes at a big family picnic. Uncle Bud. And Vic. Bud's always tossing horseshoes with Vic, who always wears checked slacks, even in the dead heat of summer.

SAM: I guess it evokes a more complete picture for you than for me.

RICH: Hey—what about Bud as a boy's name?

SAM: No way.

RICH: A girl's name?

SAM: Now you're talking.

RICH: What are these Yarmulke-looking things?

*He holds up a stack of breast pads.*

SAM: Breast pads. You wear them when you're nursing to prevent any embarrassing leaking stains.

RICH: *(Amazed)* They leak?

SAM: They can.

RICH: Wow. Never knew that. Those things are amazing.

*He reaches for her breasts from behind her.*

SAM: Careful. They're really sensitive.

RICH: They're really a handful, too.

*He hugs her from behind, kissing her neck.*

SAM: Tell me about it. I practically need to shoehorn these things into my bra these days. *(She turns to face him)* I wanted to buy some new ones before I left town.

RICH: Jesus. I can barely hug you with that rack.

SAM: And they're only going to get bigger, my friend.

RICH: I can't wait.

SAM: Another thing I read in one of the books was that not only do you get these freakishly large breasts, but your nipples can get really big and darker in color.

RICH: I'll need to document those changes throughout the process. Probably daily.

SAM: Of course, the cruel thing is that while my breasts grow, so too does my stomach. So my three-size jump in bra size will be linked to my five-size jump in pant size. The proportions won't do these things any justice.

RICH: I think I'll be able to handle it. May take both hands of course—

SAM: Very funny. I've got to sit down for a minute.

*RICH moves a box off a chair and SAM sits.*

RICH: You know that book Rebecca lent us? With all the pictures that track the fetal stages week by week?

SAM: Yeah.

RICH: I think that's my favorite, just because you can visually see what the growth stages are.

SAM: The pictures give me the willies, to be honest.

RICH: I'm fascinated by the whole process, and being able to see a fetus at 10 weeks, then 12, 15, 16, 22 weeks. Did you read the stuff in the back of the book? About the pictures?

SAM: No, I didn't. I really don't want to know Rich.

RICH: It's nothing grisly. They're all from some research grant through the University of California. But what gives me the creeps is, how did they get those fetuses at those stages? Were they all stillbirths? Were they—?

SAM: Rich. Please. I try not to think about it. That's why I don't spend much time reading that book.

RICH: I was emailing Andy about it and he said it kind of freaked out he and Rebecca, too. He figured there was some kind of medical black market—

SAM: *(Annoyed)* Stop already. Enough. O.K.?

RICH: *(Taken aback)* I'm sorry. I'll stop.

SAM: It's a great book, Rich. I agree. But I can too easily imagine how those pictures came to be, and it's upsetting. I've got this little nipper growing inside of me—I don't want to think too much about how those babies came to be in that book.

RICH: I'm sorry. I understand.

*RICH goes to her and kisses her on the head.*

RICH: Still feeling shitty?

SAM: Still. I'm beginning to think this part won't end.

RICH: It's getting a little better, isn't it?

SAM: A little. Not much though. Everyone says the morning sickness subsides around three months. Well, we're past three months and I don't feel the tide ebbing...

RICH: Do you want to go lay down on the couch? Or the bed?

SAM: *(Getting up and heading toward couch)* I'll use the couch. I've got all my clothes and stuff laid out on the bed.

RICH: Here. You lay down and I'll get your bag packed.

SAM: I love you like crazy, Rich, but you can't pack a suitcase to save your life. I'll do it later.

RICH: I pack a good bag.

SAM: Yeah, for some frumpy guy who doesn't care if the 15 t-shirts and shorts he's packed get wrinkled. I'll do it later.

RICH: Do you need anything?

SAM: Just my water. I left it on the table.

RICH: *(Getting her water)* Here you go sweetie.

SAM: Thanks. Any update from Andy?

RICH: I talked to him Sunday night.

SAM: Last I heard he was sleeping in their guest room and the counseling was going horribly.

*RICH is back at the boxes, taking out items and organizing them into piles.*

RICH: We only talked for a few minutes. Actually, he wanted to know if he could take you up on your babysitting offer next week. I forgot to ask you about it.

SAM: That's fine. Are he and Rebecca going out? Like on a date?

RICH: No. He's going to some farewell dinner with people from work, and Rebecca's going to be out of town.

SAM: Let me guess: Boston?

RICH: That's right. A two-day trip. Andy said he was going to take David and fly to Boston and follow her around like in some cheesy made-for-TV movie.

SAM: He's not really?

RICH: No. Although I wouldn't put it past him. He's got that pit bull jaw lock when he gets on to something.

SAM: I haven't talked to Rebecca in a couple of weeks. We've emailed a little, but it's all defensive and kind of nasty side-comments about Andy.

RICH: From the little that he's told me, it sounds like this marriage counseling is only fueling everybody's anger.

SAM: Rebecca said that she feels like it's an hour of Andy accusing her of everything she's ever done and him just denying everything she brings up. And she's pretty sure that Andy's hitting on the counselor.

RICH: That's rich. Rebecca's a major league flirt. Has been since I first met her.

SAM: Doesn't mean Andy isn't hitting on the woman. Could be some kind of twisted retaliation thing.

RICH: Could be. Andy can be petty like that. Even if Rebecca didn't have an affair—Andy's got it in his head now.

SAM: You say that as if she did.

RICH: Well...I know you said she denied it when you asked her about it, but based on what Andy told me, I'm still very skeptical.

SAM: Basing that kind of accusation on Andy's sense of smell is pretty suspect to me.

RICH: It wasn't just that. It was the trip that Rebecca's boss wasn't even aware of, the repeated long hours. What about Andy coming home and finding her taking a shower in the middle of the workday?

SAM: I don't know, Rich. It doesn't prove anything. I just think that until Rebecca says, "Yes, I've been having an affair," I have to take her at her word. That's all we really have—people's word.

RICH: I know. And it's really none of my business what went on. It's just that Andy's one of my oldest friends, difficult as he may be at times. He's not one to just falsely accuse people of things. Even when one of his old girlfriends was sleeping with someone else, Andy got pissed when I tried to tell him about it. I'm his friend and he got pissed at *me* for bringing the bad news. He wouldn't believe it until she actually copped to it.

SAM: But this is different. This is the person he chose to spend the rest of his life with, to have a family with. It's more emotionally complex.

RICH: You know that Rebecca started dating Andy while she was still living with that Don guy?

SAM: I've heard that story.

RICH: It wasn't until Andy kind of forced the issue with her that she broke it off with the guy and moved out. But it was like three months—

SAM: I'm sure that's running through Andy's mind as well. I don't doubt his suspicion, Rich. But there's so much at stake here that I think he has to trust Rebecca until she either admits she's been having an affair or there is some irrefutable evidence that even she couldn't deny.

RICH: Maybe. But I don't know…

SAM: Do me a favor: if at some point you get it into your head that you think I might be having an affair—which I'm not— promise me you'll accuse me only after you have more substantial evidence than how I smell.

RICH: You can't deny what the nose knows. It's our most direct-to-the-memory sense you know.

SAM: I'd need something a little more substantial, myself, before I'd go accusing you.

RICH: I'd hope so. Especially with your allergies.

SAM: You're not a very good liar anyway. I wouldn't have to do much sleuthing.

RICH: True.

SAM: I'm not sure I'd even want to know. Unless you were planning on leaving me. Then I'd like a little advance notice. A heads up. But if it was just a one-time thing, I really don't know if I'd want to find out about it.

RICH: *(Suspiciously)* Why are saying all this?

SAM: What?

RICH: This affair stuff.

SAM: I'm just talking, Rich. You don't have to worry. *(Pause)* Or maybe *I* should be worrying?

RICH: About what? *(Trying to make a joke of it)* You think I'm such a scumbag that I'd go out and have an affair while my wife's pregnant?

SAM: Not at all. If you did, with these hormones bouncing around inside me, I'd probably kill you with my bare hands if I found out.

RICH: *(Laughing a little too much)* No way I'm crossing you in this condition. I see the way you wield a paring knife.

SAM: *(Turning to face him)* And just so it's clear: what I said wasn't any form of ground rules, either.

RICH: No ground rules taken. And just so you know: should you ever have an affair, I'd want to know about it. Then I'd draw and quarter the guy.

SAM: You do love me, don't you? And in such a Medieval way.

RICH: *(Crossing to couch)* That's right, ye olde couch wench. I'll get Medieval on you right now if you don't watch yourself.

*RICH kisses SAM, and kneels next to couch.*

RICH: What time is your flight?

SAM: Insanely early. 7 a.m. *(They kiss again)* But I gotta tell you, Rich. I feel about as un-sexy as can be right now. I'm afraid I'd puke before anything else happened.

RICH: Love that dirty pillow talk. Figured I'd give it a try. *(He kisses her again)* This damn kid is already infringing on our sex life. I thought that didn't start until they were old enough to get out of bed in the middle of the night and come barging in on their parents.

SAM: I'm sure that'll happen sooner than we think.

*Beeper in kitchen goes off.*

RICH: I got it. *(Heads toward kitchen)* You want to eat out here or in the kitchen?

SAM: I suppose I can drag myself into the kitchen. *(Slowly getting up)* What's going to happen when I hit eight months and this kid weighs like 50 pounds? You'll have to wheel me around...

RICH: *(From kitchen)* I'll just borrow the maintenance dolly in the basement and cart you around on that.

SAM: All I hope is that this kid does not grow itself a huge head while in residence.

RICH: The heads in my family are well proportioned. It's your dad and brother who have the pumpkin-sized craniums.

SAM: My mom said it wasn't until after she was first pregnant with my sister that the thought of birthing a super-sized head like my dad's crossed her mind.

RICH: *(Returning from kitchen)* And I've seen his baby pictures— didn't they use a kickstand to keep that thing from slamming to the floor?

SAM: He was 60% head when he was born.

RICH: *(Back to sorting baby clothes)* He's still 60% head. No wonder he has that wrestler's neck. According to my mom, my brother's noggin' pretty much cleared the path for me. I'm pretty sure I just slipped right out... *(notices SAM watching him, getting a little teary)* What's wrong?

SAM: Nothing's wrong. I'm just...it's just these stupid hormones zipping through my body.

*RICH goes to her, wiping away her tears with a breast pad.*

RICH: Did I say something?

SAM: No, not at all. I was just watching you and thinking that you were going to be a really great dad. Like your own father, and then I thought about how happy he was when we told him about the baby—

RICH: He was a mess.

SAM: I know. It was really touching. So I thought about that and then you were checking on dinner and folding all those tiny little clothes...

RICH: What?

SAM: And nothing. I just got all teary. I warned you about what these hormones do.

RICH: *(Hugging her)* It's O.K. babe. Everything's going to be O.K. The kid'll have a tiny little head crammed full with a really big brain.

SAM: *(Giggling, sniffling)* I think I snotted on your shirt.

RICH: So long as it was a drip and not a wipe.

*RICH steps back, with his hands on her shoulders.*

RICH: I don't care how weepy or snotty you are—I still love you like crazy, Sam. And we're going to be great parents with a really great kid.

SAM: I know, I know. *(Pause)* We're going to be O.K., aren't we Rich? You and me, the baby. Everything's going to be O.K., right?

RICH: *(Taking her face in his hands)* Right.

*He kisses her. Fade to black.*

## SCENE SEVEN

*RICH and SAM'S apartment. We hear keys at the door. Door opens, RICH enters, drops his coat and bag near door, hits message button on the answering machine, and continues his getting-home routine—turning on lights, taking off shoes, etc. All the while, messages play.*

ANSWERING MACHINE: You have 8 messages. First message, 2:32 p.m. *[dead line tone. BEEP]* Next message, 3:16 p.m. *[dead line tone. BEEP.]* Next message, 4:05 p.m. *[dead line tone. BEEP.]*

RICH: Fuckin' hanger-uppers.

ANSWERING MACHINE: Next message, 6:33 p.m.

CHRIS: Please—*PLEASE* change that stupid message! This is Chris, getting back to you about Father's Day. Golf and brunch sounds good. Should I call dad or do you want to? If you haven't talked to him about his fishing expedition, then you should call him—it's a riot. Talk to ya soon. *(About to hang up, then)* Oh yeah. Ran into Andy the other day. Sounds like a regular fun house over at their place. But I want to ask you about something he said to me. Something about that concert you skipped out on. Give me a call.

ANSWERING MACHINE: BEEP. Next message, 6:50 p.m. *[dead line tone. BEEP.]* Next message, 8:12 p.m. *[dead line tone. BEEP.]* Next message, 10:02 p.m.

SAM: Hi Rich. It's me. Got your message. Nothing major to report here. Besides feeling like shit on stick, my presentation went well. I think we're in. Anyway, it's 11 here. I'll be up maybe another half an hour or so, so give me a call if you can. Oh yeah—did you call your brother about Father's Day? I'm guessing it'll be the usual golf and brunch thing, but figure out timing and all that, O.K. That's about it. I miss you. If I don't talk to you tonight, I'll see you tomorrow night. No working late tomorrow, you hear? O.K. Good night sweetie. I love you.

ANSWERING MACHINE: BEEP. Next message, 10:29 p.m. *[dead line tone]* End of messages.

*RICH is on the couch, pulling fast food out of a bag. He goes to the stereo and puts on some music. Coltrane's* "Giant Steps" *begins playing. He turns on the TV and mutes the volume. There's a tentative knock on the door. Not sure if he heard it, RICH turns down the music a little. Another tentative knock on the door. RICH crosses to door and looks through peephole. He freezes. He turns from door, unsure what to do. He looks again through the peephole. A less tentative knock on the door. RICH steels himself, turns the knob, and slowly opens the door. It's CASSANDRA.*

RICH: Cassandra. Hello.

CASS: Hello.

RICH: What's up? Why are you here?

CASS: Is she here?

RICH: Sam? No, she's not. She's out of town. On her way back from out of town, actually. She's probably landed at the airport already. *(Checks his watch)* Definitely landed. Probably on her way home already. What's up?

CASS: I tried to call to make sure she wasn't here.

RICH: So you were all the hang ups.

CASS: Yes. A hang up. Yes, that's me.

RICH: *(Gingerly)* Cassandra, I thought I was pretty straightforward with you about Sam and I when you came to my office—

CASS: I'm pregnant.

*RICH stands in stunned silence. CASS steps into the apartment.*

CASS: Did you hear me, Rich?

*RICH turns from CASSANDRA. He walks, as if in a daze, toward the couch.*

CASS: *(After a long pause)* I'm pregnant, Rich.

*Fade to black. End of Act One.*

## ACT TWO
## SCENE ONE

*RICH'S dad's house. Kitchen. RICH and his DAD are having coffee
and cutting pieces off of a coffee cake between them. RICH'S dad
is still in his robe, telling a story. He is bright red from sunburn.*

DAD: *(Acting out story)* So the bobber just disappears.
Completely disappears into the water. And about a second later, I
feel this incredible yank—pulls me ass over tit right into the back
wall of the boat. With the pole wedged between the boat and my
shoulder here *(grabs his collar bone)*. I can feel the pole wanting
to fly right out of the boat.

RICH: Where's Alice and the guy who owns the boat?

DAD: She's sunbathing at the front of the boat with her iPod on.
Bob—Captain Bob—and his girlfriend Crystal—Rich, this chick
was maybe 25, *maybe*, and Captain Bob's about my age—they
were below sleeping. They started every day with about six Bloody
Marys, so by mid-afternoon, they would crash for a couple of
hours. Really nice people. Captain Bob cracked me up. Real
fisherman, you know? Salty—"the Salty Dog" Crystal called him.

RICH: So this was like one of those professional fishing
excursions?

DAD: No. He's an old friend of Alice's. He just really loves fishing
and being out on his boat. He runs a mortgage brokerage in
Miami. Super guy. You'd really like him.

RICH: Why do you say that?

DAD: Cause you would. He's very mellow, kind of a dry sense of
humor—

RICH: Sounds like Chris would like him.

DAD: You're right. Chris would like him. He reminded me of
Chris a little bit. But I still think you'd like Captain Bob. He's a

really fun guy.

RICH: So what happened?

DAD: Oh yeah. So I'm pinned against the back of the boat and I can feel this pole trying to fly out of my hands, so I grab it with one hand kind of above my head like this *(physically acting it out)* and I'm wedging it against the back of the boat with my shoulder like this. I'm basically using the pole to try to stand up at this point. The whole time this pole is surging, then going a little slack, then surging even stronger. I figured I had a whale on the end of this thing. Or Jaws—something huge. So I'm slowly trying to stand up, wedging this pole against the boat and holding on with my one hand for dear life—

RICH: How come you didn't yell for help?

DAD: I did. The whole time I'm yelling "Bob! Crystal! Alice!"

RICH: "Salty Dog!"

DAD: That too. "Salty Dog!" I was yelling, but they didn't hear me. So I finally get on my feet and I'm holding the middle of the pole with both hands now—it had gone slack for a few seconds so I figured I'd try to make it over to Bob's fishing chair where I could strap the pole into a holder. As I'm gripping the pole, still pushing it up against the back edge of the boat for support, the line surges again really hard. So the front of the pole bends way over toward the water, and the reel—

RICH: I think I know where this is going—

DAD: *(Starting to laugh)* Slams up right between my legs! THWACK!

RICH: Ouch!

DAD: Tell me about it. I actually saw stars. And it felt like my balls were wedged up here in my throat.

RICH: I'm surprised you didn't pass out.

DAD: The reel hit me so hard in the crotch that it tore into my pants. So I'm standing there for like a split second, stars twinkling in my eyes, my eyes watering, and the pole surges again—taking me crotch first into the back of the boat. *(Laughs)* It was like something out of a cartoon, you know? It was all I could do to get my hands around the pole—

RICH: Excuse me?

DAD: The fishing pole, smart guy. It was all I could do to get a grip on it and rip it away from my pants. So there I am, woozy from this crack to the balls, still seeing stars, trying to get this reel that's pinned me to the back of the boat unhooked from my pants. *(Laughs again)* I really wish someone would've filmed it because it must've been hysterical to see.

RICH: You should've just let whatever was at the other end of the line have the damn pole.

DAD: So the line goes slack again, I tear the thing out from my pants, and dash as fast as I can to Bob's chair and slam this pole into the holder thingy and clamp it down. And as I'm sitting there, the pain actually registered, and I yelled louder than I'd ever yelled in my whole life. "FFFFFUUUUCCCCKKKKK!" It was the most satisfying curse I've ever had.

RICH: Didn't that wake everybody up?

DAD: Eventually. I must've screamed about five times. I'm sitting in the chair checking myself for blood through the gaping hole in the crotch of my shorts. I notice that the line looks really slack. Just kind of waving in the wind. So I start reeling it in, my nuts still throbbing in pain, and I see the busted end of the line come flipping over the edge of the boat.

RICH: Oh man.

DAD: Needless to say, I think people in Southern Mexico heard me yelling at that fish. "You son of a bitch!" I was like a crazy person. Standing at the back of the boat, yelling at some fish and shaking one hand at the water and holding my nuts with the other hand. *(Cracks up laughing)* I'm telling you, I wish someone would've filmed it. Could've been on one of those funniest home video shows.

RICH: So you have an honest to goodness "one that got away" fish story.

DAD: I do. It got away and almost took me with it.

RICH: Looks like you got a little sunburned, too.

DAD: A little? You should've seen me right when we got back to town. This is mild looking.

RICH: When Chris told me you were going on this trip, we kind of joked about you burning up out on a boat in the ocean. Still won't wear the sunscreen, huh?

DAD: I did wear it. Alice wouldn't let me out on the deck of the boat without the stuff gobbed all over me. This burn happened the day we were coming home. Alice was out shopping, and I was hanging at the boat with Bob and Crystal. They went to run some errands, and I fell asleep sitting on the deck.

RICH: For how long?

DAD: Two hours. High noon. The motion of the waves on the boat just lulled me to sleep. I never slept better in my life than when we were on that boat.

RICH: Looks painful.

DAD: It was. I had some bad blistering on my stomach and chest. Captain Bob woke me up when he got back. My skin felt crispy.

RICH: I'm still amazed you went on a fishing vacation. Chris and I thought you always hated fishing.

DAD: Oh no. When I was a kid, I *loved* to fish.

RICH: So how come you never seemed that interested in it when Chris and I wanted to go when we were kids?

DAD: I took you kids fishing.

RICH: Yeah, maybe four or five times.

DAD: Well, part of it was time, Rich. There was always so much going on and so much to do on the weekends. You and Chris had so many sports teams going, and your mother and I always had something or another going on in the neighborhood, or with the house, or with her parents when they were living with us.

RICH: I guess I always figured you just didn't like doing fishing.

DAD: Do you remember the times we went fishing?

RICH: Yeah. A handful of times.

DAD: Do you remember how those trips went?

RICH: I remember the one time when Chris hooked you in the leg.

DAD: The *one* time? And just Chris?

RICH: I never hooked you in the leg.

DAD: True—you got me the last time we went fishing. Right here (*points to a spot on his neck*). You don't remember that?

RICH: I do. But that was an accident.

DAD: (*Laughs*) I know it was an accident, Rich. But that's why I stopped taking you two fishing. There were always accidents. You guys goofed off more than you ever fished. I think every time we went on a little fishing excursion, someone—usually me—got hooked. You hooked Chris right here *(points to a spot near the corner of his right eye)*. Amazing it didn't catch him in the eyeball.

RICH: I don't think there was a hooking every time we went.

DAD: Ask your mother. That last time, when you hooked me in the neck, we came back to the house and I told your mother that that was the last time I take you two fishing. See, when I was a kid, I went fishing with my grandfather—the only grandparent I ever knew. He loved to fish. And I was his only grandchild who really liked fishing, so we would go a lot during the summer. It was really special to me. Me and my grandpa going out early in the morning, fishing and talking. Not even talking all that much. But you know what my family life was like, Rich. My father was an alcoholic, so for me, the more time I could be out of the house the better. And every summer, from the time I was about eight until my grandfather died when I was 14, I went fishing with him almost every weekend. I looked forward to summer so much as a kid because I could get up early, go outside for the whole day, and come back at dusk for dinner and barely have to see my dad. So for me, fishing is kind of a special thing. It's a hobby I loved as a kid, so when I took my own kids out to fish, and there was so much noise and mayhem and someone always getting hooked... it's like I didn't want to ruin one of the few outdoor activities that meant something to me.

RICH: *(Pause)* I didn't realize it was something so special, Dad.

DAD: You were a kid. There was no way to explain what it meant to me and have you really understand. And all you were doing was what kids do—goofing off with their brother.

RICH: After this big fishing trip you just had, maybe we should go out and try it again. No hooking, I promise.

DAD: Sure. Though it *was* your brother who did most of the hooking. But sure—we could go out fishing sometime. Do you like fishing?

RICH: I don't know. Haven't done it since I was a teenager on a camping trip. I might like it more now. The quiet is nice sometimes.

DAD: Sure is. *(Pause. Looks at RICH, considering him a moment.)* How are you Rich?

RICH: Fine. Doing fine. There's so much going on at work and so much to read and learn about this whole baby thing that I've kind of been on autopilot trying to balance everything.

DAD: So what's up?

RICH: Not a lot, really.

DAD: *(Pauses, looking at him.)* I don't buy it.

RICH: Don't buy it? Don't buy what?

DAD: You've been quite distracted lately, Rich. Every time we've talked.

RICH: Like I said, there's a lot going on right now.

DAD: You said that. But I know you, Rich. You're my son. You've always had a lot going on. But here it's *(looks at clock on wall)* 7:30 a.m. on a Sunday morning and you're sitting in my kitchen. And our tee time isn't for almost two hours.

RICH: I can't come by a little early—

DAD: Rich, you're like me. You're *never* early for anything. Something's on your mind. You know you can talk to me.

RICH: *(Looking away)* I know. I know. And there is…there is something I wanted to talk to you about.

DAD: What is it, Rich?

RICH: *(Standing, moving nervously.)* I don't really know how to talk about this, Dad. Especially with you.

DAD: Just talk. I always listen.

RICH: I know, it's just...it's just that it's something I'm very ashamed of...I haven't been able to talk to anybody about this...

DAD: Go on, Rich. I've always been a safe house, you know that.

RICH: I know. I know. *(Pause. Looking down, his voice unsteady.)* O.K. Well, here goes. I had a...I met this...I slept with someone. A woman.

DAD: O.K. *(Pause)* Do you want to tell me what happened?

RICH: I ran into this woman at a coffee shop and one thing led to another and we ended up sleeping together.

DAD: When did this—

RICH: It was before Sam got pregnant. We got pregnant.

DAD: And you've been walking around with this eating away at you ever since.

RICH: Yes. Been a few months.

DAD: Why'd you do it?

RICH: I don't know, Dad. I really don't know. I wasn't looking to go out and have this little thing—

DAD: An affair.

RICH: A tryst. It was more like a tryst. I haven't seen her since. Haven't even tried to.

DAD: So why do you think you did it?

RICH: I don't know. I love Sam like crazy. We weren't having any typical marriage problems or anything. It just...happened.

DAD: Things don't just happen, Rich. You know that. Maybe that's what you need to figure out. Why you did it.

RICH: I've been trying to, Dad. I don't know if it's because we've been together for so many years and I was just curious, or if I wanted to prove some sick shit to myself, like I was still attractive to women and could still have that kind of effect on them.

DAD: What kind of effect?

RICH: You know. *That* kind of effect. An allure. Something physically alluring.

DAD: A conquest?

RICH: I don't think so. Maybe. I don't know. I met her at this coffee shop, started chatting, and I found her so interesting and so charismatic...we had some coffee, then some dinner, wine, and before I knew what I was doing I was inviting her to our apartment.

DAD: I take it Sam was out of town.

RICH: No, she was there, Dad.

DAD: You don't have to get shitty with me, Rich.

RICH: I'm sorry. Sorry. *(Pauses)* Sam was out of town, yes. But even then, even when I was aware of how messed up this situation was getting, I still wasn't able to stop it. It's like I wanted to see how far I would go with it.

DAD: You found out alright.

RICH: I know that sounds twisted, but that's kind of what I was thinking in the back of my head at the time. *(Pause)* And I got my answer...

DAD: Does Sam know?

RICH: No. No, she doesn't know.

DAD: Do you want her to know?

RICH: That's what I'm going over and over again in my head. I want to tell her. To be completely honest with her. Cause I hate this feeling of harboring this lie.

DAD: But you don't—or feel you can't—tell her now.

RICH: Exactly. If she wasn't pregnant—we weren't pregnant—I probably would've told her already. But I can't now.

DAD: What would telling her do?

RICH: What do you mean?

DAD: I mean, what would telling her do for you?

RICH: *(Unsure)* It would mean I was completely honest with her. Even about something really awful like this.

DAD: Would that make you feel better? That she knew?

RICH: Yeah. I think so. I'm not sure I get what you're asking.

DAD: I'm asking why you feel the compulsion to tell her about this. What it will mean for you. Because you know what it will mean to her. That her husband slept with another woman. And all the betrayal and anger and suspicion that entails.

RICH: Are you saying I shouldn't tell her about this? Ever?

DAD: That's your call. But speaking from experience, you have to think about what this will mean to Sam. What it will do to her feelings, her thoughts about your relationship, even her love for you. It's not just about *you* getting this off your chest. It affects her, too.

RICH: Of course it affects her too. That's why I feel like I should tell her and be completely honest about it. Not now though. I can't now. I just can't.

DAD: So why drum it up six months from now, a year from now? When would it be the "right" time? And what would be the point?

RICH: *(Sitting down, staring at his father)* I'm...I'm kind of shocked to hear this from you, Dad.

DAD: What were you expecting me to say?

RICH: I'm not sure what I expected, but I didn't expect this.

DAD: What do want me to say? That this is a horrible, terrible thing and you better go tell poor Sam right now? Or did you want something more parental: Rich, I'm very, very disappointed in you. How could you do such a terrible thing?

RICH: No, I guess—

DAD: Did you want a punishment of some kind?

RICH: No, of course not.

DAD: Then what?

RICH: I wanted to tell someone that I knew would listen and not pass judgment.

DAD: And?

RICH: And...and maybe I'd like some advice. Some direction.

DAD: I don't know if I can really give you either of those, Rich. My experience in these matters wasn't very good. But I must say this: I don't pass any judgment on you about this, Rich. People do things that aren't so nice sometimes. That's the way life is. Now, I'd be lying if I said that, as your father, I wasn't disappointed by this. Or even a little hurt for Sam. Because I think the world of her. But one thing you learn as a dad is that your kids are going to make bad decisions and there's not much of anything you can do about it. This was a bad decision, Rich. You know that. There's nothing I can really say to change that. You have to live with it. And this turmoil you're feeling…that's the price of a bad decision. No parent or friend or spouse can absolve you of that. If you're looking to be absolved or forgiven by some parental figure, I'm not the one. If you were religious I'd say talk to your priest. *(Pause)* Maybe this is the worst thing you've ever done in your life? But you've done it; it's part of you now. It's a scar you wear, whether anybody else ever knows about it or not.

*RICH considers what his father has just said.*

RICH: *(Slowly)* So is this like some advanced level of parental disappointment? Throwing it back on the kid.

DAD: I guess. I can't be the parent to you anymore, Rich. It's really not fair. Or possible. You'll always be my youngest son, and I'll always have in my memory all the images of you growing up, but you're a grown man now. It's not fair for me to still view you as a child. And it's not fair of you to view me only as "the dad." We're both more than that now. So when you come to me with this situation, I can only give you my honest reaction. You made a really lousy decision, son. Now what are you going to do about it? How are you going to live with it?

RICH: I don't know, Dad. I really don't know what to do.

DAD: You need to really think through what telling Sam about this will mean to her. And you may decide it's the right thing to do—to tell her. That's fine. That would be the right decision for you. *(Pause)* You know your mother never said anything to me about her affairs. I discovered that information. Which made it a very different thing: I had the knowledge of this thing that she thought she was hiding from me. I rolled it over in my head for quite a while until I finally decided that I had to do what I had to do.

RICH: You told her you knew.

DAD: I did. I'm not going to rehash all that now, but I did. Because I felt I had to. And I sometimes wonder what would've happened had I never said a word. But ultimately I know I did the best thing. I'm certain of that now.

RICH: I guess the reason I feel the need to tell Sam about this is because our whole relationship has been based on being honest with each other. I almost feel like I'm lying to her every day that goes by that I don't tell her.

DAD: I understand that, Rich, but I think that honesty thing is a bit overblown.

RICH: Overblown?

DAD: That didn't come out right. Yes, honesty is the best policy—

RICH: That's what you always said.

DAD: And I believe it. But honesty to an eight year old, even a 14 year old, is more black and white. You know how grey things can be sometimes. The world is not black and white. This is nothing I need to tell you at this point in your life. But being honest, at least as I've found in my experience, gets quite grey at times. And this is a situation where it's really grey. The black and white answer may not be the best answer.

RICH: I understand that, dad. But to me, trust is a really elemental issue between two people. It's the most important thing.

DAD: *(Cutting Rich a piece of coffee cake)* Remember Mrs. Anderson who lived next door?

RICH: Yeah. The Andersons. Their daughter was Chris' age.

DAD: A little older I think. I know Chris had a huge crush on her. But you remember Mr. Anderson died when you were a kid?

RICH: I do. I think I was like 9 or 10.

DAD: Massive heart attack. Seemingly healthy guy. He was a little older than Ruth—than Mrs. Anderson.

RICH: Mrs. Anderson was one of the nicest parents on that block.

DAD: Very sweet lady. But a few years after her husband died—maybe it was more like five or six, I don't really remember—I was in the house on a really nice summer afternoon—

RICH: The Anderson's house?

DAD: No. Our house. I was in our bedroom fixing something. Probably that closet door that would never quite stay closed.

RICH: And that you fixed at least once a year.

DAD: Seemed like it. Anyway, I was in the bedroom, and our window faced the Anderson's bedroom window, and I heard what sounded like someone crying. Just a kind of quiet crying. I leaned over near the window and could hear it a little better, and it was coming from Mrs. Anderson's bedroom across the way. I knew she sometimes got down about her husband having died, especially after Emily went off to college.

RICH: She was probably very alone in the house.

DAD: She was—she said as much. Anyway, kneeling by the bedroom window and listening to her cry on a beautiful Saturday afternoon, it made me feel a little sad for her. But as I sat there by the window for a minute, I realized she wasn't crying.
RICH: What was she doing?

DAD: I'm getting there. I looked through our window across toward hers. It's wide open, just a screen—and I can see into the bedroom. I hear these little noises. And I notice there are two legs—I can't even believe I'm telling you this, Rich. I've never told anybody about this.

RICH: *(Cautiously)* About what?

DAD: Well, when I looked across the window there, I saw these two legs…a nice pair of women's legs, kind of open there on the bed. You know what I'm saying?

RICH: I…think…so. Are you saying you saw Mrs. Anderson—?

DAD: Yes. She was. And what I thought was someone crying was exactly the opposite. Not sad sounds at all, y'know.

RICH: She was…?

DAD: Yeah.

RICH: And you watched her through the window?

DAD: Yeah. For a little bit. I'd never seen anything like that before—

RICH: *(Standing and walking about the room)* WHOA! Hold on. TMI. TMI.

DAD: TMI?

RICH: Too much information, Dad. That's *way* more than I think I should know about my father. That he watched the neighbor lady through the window—

DAD: TMI then. I'm sorry. I didn't realize it would offend you.

RICH: It doesn't offend me, it's just…I don't know that I want to know something like that about my dad. It's too weird.

DAD: Alright, alright. Pipe down. I was telling you that story for a reason.

RICH: That's kind of bordering on peeping tom stuff, Dad.

DAD: What are you talking about? I wasn't prowling around her window. I heard something, I looked out the window, and there she was. Plain as day. With the sun shining in the window right on—

RICH: I got the picture, dad. You don't have to describe it in any more detail.

DAD: You're going to tell me that you never saw someone naked through a window? Never in your life did you happen across a situation like this? Not as a teenager, not in college—

RICH: That's not the point.

DAD: Answer the question, Rich.

RICH: It doesn't matter. This is about my dad peeping into a neighbor's window and how freakin' weird that is.

DAD: The point is I never told anybody—including your mother—that this was going on. I never really saw the point in—

RICH: Wait. This was going on? You mean it happened more than once?

DAD: It happened a number of times.

RICH: Oh man. Dad.

DAD: "Oh man, Dad" what? Mrs. Anderson knew what was going on—

RICH: What?!

DAD: She knew what was going on. She saw me through the window one summer afternoon. I thought she'd start screaming or something but she didn't. She moved to the edge of the bed close to the window—

RICH: STOP. Please. I don't want to hear anymore. This is getting *way* too weird.

DAD: It was a little odd, but where was the harm? We were two grown people. We were both comfortable with it. And it wasn't hurting anybody.

RICH: It's hurting my head right now.

DAD: Oh come on, Rich. If one of your friends told you the same story, would you be so offended by it?

RICH: I don't know. I'd still think it was weird.

DAD: You know, over the years you've complained that I talk more to Chris about personal things in my life than I do you. And you're right—I do. But now I'm talking to you man to man, as I would to a friend or your brother, and you're acting like some embarrassed teenager.

RICH: This is the personal story you choose to share with me?

DAD: It is a corker, isn't it? Forget the story Rich—

RICH: How can I forget it? I'm going to have nightmares about it.

DAD: Very funny. But the sex part of the story is not the point. The point is I never told anybody about it because I never felt the need to. Telling your mother about it would have done nothing positive to our lives. True, I would've been more honest with her, she would've known what kind of offbeat thing I was capable of—

RICH: Off-beat's putting it lightly—

DAD: But it would've had nothing but a very negative impact on our marriage. It had nothing to do with your mother. I wasn't doing it to hurt her. I wasn't doing it to prove anything to her. Or to me. As I found out a few years after this incident with Mrs. Anderson, your mother'd already had an affair with some guy from the PTA board. So it wasn't like I was getting back at her. It happened, between two adult people, not even in the same room. What was the point in saying anything to your mother about it? *(Waits for an answer)* There was no point. See, Rich, just because you're married to someone doesn't mean you can't have anything just for yourself. Just kept to yourself.

RICH: Our situations are a little different, dad.

DAD: I know they are, but I'm saying this—

RICH: For one, I was actually in the room with this person.

DAD: Good for you, Rich. You were. And you had sex with her. But unless you're thinking there's more to this one-night stand with this woman, there's a great similarity between our two situations: what are you going to do with this information that you have? On purely moral grounds, if you want to look at it that way, you beat me hands down. So the stakes are higher, true. But you're in control of this situation, Rich. Consider all the factors before you act on what you decide.

RICH: And that's the crux of the problem. All these things are just flying around in my head.

*Sound of a car outside.*

DAD: That must be Chris.

RICH: *(Looking at his watch)* Bet it is. Hey dad: what I told you here, this is just between you and me, O.K.?

DAD: Of course, Rich. And my story too.

RICH: I don't even know if I *could* tell anyone that story.

*CHRIS enters.*

CHRIS: Morning all. Happy Father's Day. *(Hugging his dad)* Ready for another round of dad teaches his sons a few new swears?

DAD: I think I could probably learn a few choice terms from you two.

CHRIS: Happy Father-to-be Day to you, Rich.

RICH: *(To DAD)* You should get dressed Dad. We should get going here.

DAD: Just give me a minute. You guys figure out who's driving and then grab my clubs. They're in the garage there.

*DAD exits.*

RICH: I take it dad gave you the whole story of his one that got away.

CHRIS: Oh yeah. It took him a good half an hour to tell me the whole thing. It probably gets longer and more embellished with each telling.

RICH: And that's a pretty sweet sunburn, too.

CHRIS: Lobster-ish. *(Moving closer to RICH)* I have to ask you something, Rich. Before dad comes back down.

RICH: What is it?

CHRIS: Ran into Andy a couple of weeks ago. Sounds like he and Rebecca are in bad shape.

RICH: Are they ever. Did he tell you what was going on? Or what he thinks is going on.

CHRIS: Yeah—he gave me the run-down. Sounds nasty. But that's not what I wanted to ask you about. Andy made some reference to how much you liked the concert he couldn't make. The concert you blew off. Remember?

RICH: That's weird.

CHRIS: I thought so too. Kind of threw me a little bit at first. So I played along. But now I'm asking you: why would he have the impression that you'd gone to that concert? He said you even raved about what a great show it was.

RICH: No idea. I told him *you* raved about it. Because you did. Maybe you misheard him.

CHRIS: *(Suspiciously)* No. I didn't mishear him. He even mentioned specific songs you raved about.

*There's an awkward pause between them. We hear the sound of DAD approaching from another room.*

CHRIS: Something stinks, Rich. I heard Andy perfectly clear.

DAD: *(From other room)* I'm going to need to stop on the way home to pick up a couple of things from the store.

RICH: *(Happy to change the subject)* No problem Dad, we can stop. *(To Chris)* Why don't I drive?

CHRIS: Fine. But Rich, why does Andy think you went to that show? You told me you were home sick as a dog, remember?

RICH: What's with you? Back off it, O.K.?

*DAD enters the kitchen wearing a very loud tropical-patterned shirt.*

DAD: C'mon guys, we've got to go. Tee times at 9, right?

CHRIS: More like 9:30. I factored in the Dad-Rich time challenge. However, what I didn't factor in was that shirt. I can't golf with someone wearing a shirt like that.

DAD: What? What's wrong with this shirt?

RICH: I'll grab your clubs and meet you outside—that thing's scaring me.

*RICH exits quickly.*

CHRIS: I think the question is what's *right* with that shirt?

DAD: *(Heading toward door)* These things were all the rage down in the Keys. It's silk.

CHRIS: Silk, cotton, cardboard—I still can't really hear you over the shrieking volume.

DAD: *(As they leave)* Maybe it'll distract you when you're swinging and give me an advantage.

CHRIS: It's going to be hard not to aim at the thing.

*CHRIS stops at the door and picks up bottle of sunscreen from a nearby table.*

CHRIS: Hey Dad. You forgot your sunscreen.

DAD: *(From outside)* Leave it. I can't stand the feel of that stuff on my skin.

CHRIS sets it down and closes the door. Door opens quickly again and CHRIS grabs the sunscreen.

*Fade to black.*

## SCENE TWO

*RICH'S office. His headset's on and he's at his computer.*

RICH: That's the idea, Marvin. Start the campaign local, then go regional. Ease into the national effort. So everyone's on board with the "so good you have to sneak them" idea? *(Pause)* That's great. I knew once you spent some time with the mock-ups we put together it would be much clearer. *(Pause)* That is a good one. Appeals to the cookie-lover in all of us. *(Pause)* Oh really? These are your ideas? Ideas that came out of the meeting? *(Pause)* Sure. Great. Let's have 'em.

*Pause. A look of confusion creeps over his face the more he hears.*

O.K. So the kid is hiding in a closet eating a cookie. To hide from his brother. Sure, sure, I get it. But isn't a closet the kind of a place a kid *would* hide from a brother anyway? I know I did when I was a kid. *(Pause)* I see. Well, part of the reason that ad with the CEO turned around in his chair and sneaking a cookie during a big board meeting works is because it's not the kind of place you'd expect someone to be eating a cookie. See? *(Pause)* Well, yeah, you're right. Not every kid would hide in a closet to sneak a cookie. Let me work on that one a little, do some brainstorming. I think we can— *(Pause)* Oh. O.K. Let's hear it.

*Pause. Rich drops his head, shaking it slowly, incredulous.*

Yeah, yeah. I get it Marvin. A man hiding under a box, eating a cookie. I get it alright. How would you see him hiding under the box eating a cookie? *(Pause)* See, that's the tough part. You've got to be able to see what he's doing to get it.

*Door bursts open and ANDY enters, out of breath, agitated.*

ANDY: I fucking knew it!

*He sees RICH on phone and begins pacing office.*

RICH: *(Gesturing for ANDY to be quiet)* No, no Marvin. I left my office door open. Big deadline here today. Things get a little tense. So let us do a little brainstorming on these ideas and see—*(Pause)* I don't know if they're quite there yet. But potential, yes, definitely. Especially the one with the guy under the box. Wonder where the box would be? Let me get back to you later in the week. But I'm glad everyone liked the spreads we sent—*(Pause)* Spreads. The ad mock-ups we sent you. That's what we call them. *(Pause)* Sure is a lot of lingo in the marketing game, Marvin. You're right. We'll talk by Friday, O.K.? *(Pause)* So do I, Marvin. It's been hot as Hades down here too. I'll call you by Friday, O.K.

ANDY: *(From near the door, loudly)* Rich—we need you in this meeting right now. Lots of spreads to approve.

RICH: *(Giving ANDY a thumbs up)* Well, gotta go, Marvin. You heard it—big spread meeting. I'll get back to you in a few days. *(Pause. He starts pulling at his hair)* Yeah, boy, the Cubs are really struggling this season aren't they? But—

ANDY: NOW RICH! Let's move it!

RICH: That's the boss, Marvin. I'll talk to you soon. *(Hangs up without waiting for a response. To ANDY)* Thanks dude. That old codger can small talk you to death. Nice enough guy but—

ANDY: *(At RICH'S desk)* I fucking knew it, Rich. I knew she was sleeping with this fucker from Boston.

RICH: You know for sure? Did she cop to it?

ANDY: No she didn't cop to it. She's a fucking liar, Rich. You think she'd have the decency to just admit it?

RICH: Then how do you know?

ANDY: I just came from her office. They were there practically doing it right there. I knew it, Rich. I told you, didn't I? I knew she was screwing around with this guy.

RICH: Calm down, O.K. Calm down. Tell me what happened. From the beginning.

ANDY: Calm down? CALM DOWN?! How the hell am I supposed to calm down after this—after catching my wife red-handed with some other guy? Tell me to calm down...I came over here so I wouldn't fucking kill both of them right there in the restaurant.

RICH: What restaurant? What are you talking about? I thought you said you saw them at her office—

ANDY: I decided to go over to her office on my lunch break. I knew this fucker from Boston was in town again, so I thought I might go by her office at lunch, maybe go out for lunch with my wife, maybe meet this all important fucker from Boston—

RICH: Maybe catch Rebecca in the act—

ANDY: Why not? It was a fishing expedition. O.K.? A really fucked-up fishing expedition. But I hooked the big one, Rich. *(Almost more to himself)* I fucking knew it!

RICH: So what happened? You went to her office—

ANDY: I didn't even get to her office. I'm walking up Dearborn, kind of plotting out what exactly I was going to say. Rebecca was going to be suspicious of me "stopping by." So I'm standing at the corner of Dearborn and Madison and I see someone who looks like Rebecca in the window of this restaurant. I did a double take—it *was* Rebecca. And sitting across from her is some guy. Goofy looking fucker, but it's through the window, and I'm kind of in shock to actually see her there with this guy. So I cross the street and kind of stand behind this car that's parked outside the restaurant, making sure it's Rebecca. Which it was. And I notice she's holding hands with this guy—they're playing some fucking little hand holding game, and Rebecca's all giggly and smiling and flirty. You know how she gets.

RICH: Not really, but—

ANDY: We'll I do. She's got this certain flirty smile she uses with men. So I stood there for about 20 minutes, first in shock, then I wanted to storm into the restaurant and stab the two of them with a fucking fork. Then I thought about David and I just wanted to cry. She was all over this guy, Rich. Holding hands, touching his face, making out with him. FUCK!

RICH: You've got to keep it down, Andy. I know you're pissed, but you can't—

ANDY: *(Nearing tears)* I can't believe I watched her kissing someone else. I can't believe it, Rich. And she kept looking at him like he was the most exciting thing she'd ever seen. That was her look for *me*. That was the look I fell in love with, Rich. For *me*.

*He slumps against the wall and covers his face, sobbing.*

ANDY: I can't believe she was kissing someone else...

*RICH turns to Andy, unsure what to do.*

RICH: I'm sorry, Andy. I really am sorry.

*He awkwardly puts his hand on ANDY'S shoulder. ANDY looks up, wiping his eyes.*

ANDY: So much for marriage counseling, huh?

*They both laugh awkwardly.*

ANDY: You know, I've known this was happening for a while, even though Rebecca refused to admit it, but to actually see it...to actually see your wife with another man...I can't take it, Rich. I can't take it. I don't know what to do. I don't even want to go home.

RICH: Did she see you?

ANDY: See me? No, she didn't see me. How the hell could she see me? She couldn't stop staring at this Boston fucker.

RICH: Maybe you should call her and tell her what you saw. Put the first move back on her.

ANDY: I'm sure she'll deny it. Even though I saw it with my own eyes, she'll deny it. She has all along.

RICH: Do you have to go back to your office today?

ANDY: I'm supposed to, but I can't. There's no way. I couldn't get anything done today.

RICH: Maybe you should just drive somewhere. Or take a walk. Take a really long run. Just give yourself some time to kind of think through what you want to do. How you want to approach this with Rebecca.

ANDY: I've got to pick up David at his sitter's at 5:30. Rebecca's "working late" again.

RICH: I can pick him up for you. I've done it before. I just think it's a good idea for you to take some time here and kind of settle into a calmer mindset. At least so you can go home and not just completely freak out. It's amazing what a few hours alone will do to chill you out.

ANDY: You're right. You're right. I need to let this fury and depression and HATE and everything else that's blasting through my head right now—I need to let it play out. Hopefully look at this with something like a clear head so when I do finally see her I don't explode.

RICH: If you need me to pick up David, just let me know. I can even drive him back over to your place if you need me to. *(Noticing ANDY is sobbing)* It's gonna be O.K. Andy. As shitty as it seems right now—

*ANDY looks up at RICH, tears running down his face.*

ANDY: Divorced kid, Rich. David's gonna be the Carl Bigglio of his neighborhood.

RICH: Andy, it's not going to be like that. Every other kid's a Carl Bigglio nowadays. And who says this means there has to be a divorce? Plenty of couples get through these things without—

ANDY: No. No. No. *I'll* want the divorce, Rich. It's a matter of trust. The whole thing, the whole marriage between two people is based on trust. And she totally fucked that trust. I'll never be able to trust her again. NEVER. It doesn't matter what she says, how sorry she is. It's a one strike thing, Rich.

RICH: I know that's how you feel right now, Andy, but—

ANDY: There's no but. I've been thinking about this for a while, Rich. Ever since I first suspected this affair was going on. Maybe early on, maybe before I even suspected it—if she had told me about it of her own free will, or admitted it when I first asked her about it. Maybe then I could've been more willing. If it was a one-time thing that she confessed to me, or at least had the fucking decency to admit when I asked her about it...maybe then. But not now. Not now. Not after lying to me about it and continuing to fuck this guy however many countless times over the past few months. You know when the last time Rebecca and I had sex?

RICH: You don't have to get into this Andy.

ANDY: Valentine's Day. Fucking Valentine's Day, Rich. Count 'em—that's four months, Rich. And the whole time she's—

RICH: Six, actually. Six months.

ANDY: O.K. SIX MONTHS! I haven't had sex with my wife for six months but my fucking wife has been getting it on a regular basis. How fucked up is that, Rich? *(Pause)* No. She made the decision a long time ago. She made her choice. She made her choice over and over and over again every time she slept with that FUCKER FROM BOSTON.

RICH: Andy, please. You've got to stop shouting.

ANDY: So I don't care if she begs me to stay together, Rich. I don't care if she promises me it'll never happen again. I don't care WHAT she says. I can never trust her again. Never.

RICH: *(Pause. Then tentatively)* Um…I think that walk would be a really good thing for you right now.

ANDY: I do too. Or a drink.

RICH: You can walk while you drink—I've seen you do it before. You're good at it.

ANDY: *(Gathering himself)* It's a skill. Years of practice.

RICH: And not a single stop by a cop.

ANDY: I guess there's always a first.

RICH: You going to be O.K. by yourself?

ANDY: What? Like am I going to kill myself?

RICH: No, that's not what I meant.

ANDY: Best thing right now is for me to be by myself. I've already gotten you in trouble I'm sure.

RICH: Don't worry about it. People scream "fucker from Boston" around here all the time.

ANDY: *(Going to Rich)* Thanks Rich. I know I've been a pretty lousy friend lately—

RICH: Lately?

ANDY: Let me clarify: a particularly lousy friend lately.

RICH: It's O.K. Andy. That's what friends are for. And don't worry about David. I'll pick him up. Just let me know when you want me to bring him home.

ANDY: *(Going to door)* I will. Tell him I had to work late or something. He's used to hearing that by now.

RICH: Let me know if you need anything, O.K.? And take all the time you need.

ANDY: You know me. I need a lot of time. Thanks again, Rich.

RICH: No problem. Andy?

ANDY: *(At door)* Yeah?

RICH: I know this is going to sound really trite, but as bad as it seems right now, it isn't always going to be like this. You'll get through this.

ANDY: I know. I always do. *(Opening door to leave, then)* And yes—that was exceptionally trite. I'm leaving before you tell me the sun will come up tomorrow. I'll call you later. *(Exits)*

RICH: *(To door)* It will, Andy. It really will.

*Fade to black.*

## SCENE THREE

*Doctor's Office waiting room. RICH and CASSANDRA are seated next to each other. She is flipping through a magazine; he's looking over her shoulder.*

CASS: It's really amazing all the money that's spent on beautifying yourself. Most of this magazine is make-up ads, breast enhancements, articles on how to be more beautiful. How to better please your man. *(To RICH)* Where are the magazines that tell men how to better please their women?

RICH: Who'd buy them?

CASS: *(Looking at him)* Exactly.

RICH: Wait—what's that article?

CASS: Which one? "Nice Girls Can Be Naughty, Too."

RICH: It's got eight steps.

CASS: *(Turning page)* All of them mining the virgin-whore territory, I'm sure.

RICH: You seem to be in a good mood. Considering.

CASS: Considering what?

RICH: *(Looking at her, a little in disbelief)* Well, considering what we're doing here.

CASS: Ah yes. What *I'm* doing here.

RICH: Yes. True.

CASS: Should I be more despondent? More sullen?

RICH: No. It's just that—

CASS: It's just that what? There's really no choice here for me, Rich. Unless you have something else in mind?

RICH: No. I don't. It's the right thing to do. In this situation.

CASS: It is the right thing to do. It's the right thing to do for me, certainly. And in that, Rich, you really have no choice in the matter.

RICH: True. True again.

CASS: You don't sound so convinced.

RICH: I am convinced. Believe me—this is the right decision. It's just different to talk about something like this and then actually be making the decision to do it. To be here actually doing it.

CASS: Don't take my breeziness as an indication that this is an easy decision for me, Rich. It is not. It's been horrible, really. I never imagined I'd ever have to make this decision in my life. I'm too smart for this. This only happened to other girls I knew. Seemed there was always someone at one of the schools I attended getting pregnant. It was always someone else. *(Pause)* But here I am.

RICH: I've known a couple of people who've done the same thing. I never imagined this either.

CASS: I've had enough time to suss it all out though. So long as I don't dwell too much on what is actually going to happen. What the procedure actually does. *(Pause)* This is not something I'm proud of, Rich. I wish to god this had never happened. And I hope I don't regret this for the rest of my life. It will always be back there in the memory, floating around. But at this point in my life, there's no way I could become a mother. There's simply no way. And I don't imagine you want to be a father right now, do you?

RICH: No. No, not now. This is the right thing to do, Cassandra. *(Pause)* I know this is something I'll never forget, either.

CASS: I respect the fact that you're here with me, Rich. After the wrong phone number trick, I frankly didn't expect you to see this through with me. Which would've been fine—it's ultimately my decision, it's my body. It's something I think all women understand. Certainly more so than men.

RICH: Despite what you may think, I am a very responsible person. A very honest person. Usually.

CASS: Aren't we all. Usually? It's when it really counts, in those real crisis situations, that's when people usually falter. At least in the honesty department.

RICH: You may not believe me, of course, but that night with you was the only time in my life I've done something like that.

CASS: Slept with a woman?

RICH: No. Yes. I mean, slept with a woman other than my...you know, than the woman I was dating. Or living with.

CASS: This'll sure teach you a lesson.

RICH: Tell me about it. But that's why I gave you that wrong phone number, Cassandra. I didn't know—

CASS: Rich, please. Stop. We don't need to rehash that. It's done. I know why you did it, you know why I came to your office that day to confront you. We don't need to go over it. Frankly, if this hadn't happened, I doubt we'd ever have seen each other again.

RICH: You're probably right.

CASS: *(Returning to flipping through the magazine)* I'm just thankful this happened in a city like this. I knew a woman in Spain who went through a horrible experience—

*Nurse 1 enters.*

NURSE 1: Cassandra?

RICH: *(Nervously)* Yes.

CASS: I thought I was Cassandra today?

*She gathers her bag; follows NURSE 1.*

RICH: I'll be out here, Cassandra.

*She pauses to look over her shoulder at him.*

CASS: O.K.

*She exits behind NURSE 1. Fade to black.*

## SCENE FOUR

*Doctor's office waiting room. RICH and SAMANTHA are seated next to each other. He is flipping through a magazine; she's looking over his shoulder.*

RICH: These really are all beauty ads.

SAM: And lots of "How To" please your man articles. No wonder girls grow up with such feelings of inadequacy: "I'm not pretty enough, I'm not wearing the right make-up, the right clothes, I'm not sexy enough." It's such a load of crap.

RICH: Check this one: "Nice Girls Can Be Naughty, Too."

SAM: Oh, can they?

RICH: Yes they can. How do you feel about leather?

SAM: Too sweaty.

RICH: There's always the belly dancing option.

SAM: Buddy, you do not want this belly dancing at you these days.

RICH: *(Touching SAM'S stomach)* Maybe I do.

SAM: Isn't there a *People* magazine around here somewhere? It's the only time I get to catch up on gossip.

RICH: The "Nice and Naughty" thing's not doing it for you?

SAM: Not at all. But please, don't let me interfere with your fantasies.

RICH: *(Flips the magazine onto the table next to him)* That takes the joy out of it. Forget it then.

SAM: *(Patting his thigh)* We can stop and buy a copy on the way home, dear.

RICH: I suppose we should be looking at one of these baby magazines. *(Picks up magazine)*

SAM: I actually read a really interesting article in one of those at my last visit. About the essentials you need to pack for the hospital when its baby time. I've got it at home.

RICH: Here's a timely one: "Negotiating The Name Game."

SAM: What's it say?

RICH: *(Pretending to read from magazine)* "When you can't agree on a name, it's always best to defer to the dad's choice—"

SAM: It does not.

RICH: *(Laughing)* You're right—it does not.

SAM: Especially when the dad keeps coming up with these exotic names.

RICH: Exotic? These are all traditional names. Esmeralda dates back to—

SAM: Hyacinth? Ruby? Roxy? They're hooker names.

RICH: Hey—my grandmother was no hooker.

SAM: I said I liked Maeve.

RICH: But not as a first name. Then what's the point? Having this really cool middle name that nobody ever knows?

SAM: I thought you said you liked Leah as a first name?

RICH: I do. But it's a total compromise name. And not all my names are "exotic." I think Catherine is a beautiful name.

SAM: Too traditional. I knew a girl growing up named Kate who was really nasty.

RICH: See? All the regular names I suggest are "too traditional." Or you have some bad association with the name.

SAM: We've still got time. There are lots of names that we haven't even talked about.

RICH: Such as?

SAM: Well. Like for a boy, what about Zack?

RICH: Ugh. What not just call him "jerk"?

SAM: I think it's a cool name.

RICH: "Zack" is the jerky guy who likes to dole out the wedgies in the locker room. No way. That's almost as bad as "Jeb."

SAM: It's your great grandfather's name. It's kind of cool, in a retro way.

RICH: In a "Hee-Haw" kind of way. I thought we were pretty much decided on a boy's name?

SAM: Jack. Yes, but it's impossible to come up with a middle name that works with it.

RICH: I thought you liked Jack Patrick?

SAM: Kind of waning on Patrick.

RICH: I kind of liked your grandmother's maiden name: Jack Morgan.

SAM: That's not bad. Interesting at least.

RICH: I've got it! How 'bout "The Mack"? Jack "The Mack" Flaherty?

SAM: "The Mack?" What are you, high?

RICH: No one would ever mess with a kid named Jack "The Mack."

SAM: What the hell is "The Mack" anyway?

RICH: I'm not sure. But whatever it is, if you're middle name's "The Mack," you got it.

SAM: Sounds like a guy in a prison movie.

RICH: The Mack bunks with Stevie "The Shiv" Gadzikowski. But he gets his smokes from Rust. Dude's just named Rust—nobody knows why exactly, but nobody fucks with Rust. Not even The Mack.

SAM: I'm glad you've given such thought to our child's prison future. What if it's a girl, Warden?

RICH: This is why Roxy would be such a great name. Nobody fucks with the cell block bitch Roxy.

SAM: Incarcerated, no doubt, for prostitution—because her dad named her Roxy!

RICH: Well played, well played. *(Pause) Sam*. A cell block snitch name if I ever heard one.

SAM: And this from a guy named Richard? What do they call you on the cell block?

RICH: Exactly why I'd never saddle a kid with my name. I'm in my mid-30s and people are still making "dick" jokes…

SAM: We could make this name thing half as hard by just finding out the sex.

RICH: I thought we didn't want to know?

SAM: I don't. Usually. But sometimes I think it would be nice to know—and not just for naming purposes.

RICH: Well if you really want to, we can have them tell us today. But I'd rather be surprised.

SAM: I don't know. I guess…

RICH: I can go either way, Sam.

SAM: Let's not find out. We'll just wait to see if it's Jack or Julia when it's born.

RICH: Still hooked on Julia, huh? I'm coming around to it. Very pretty name. Very elegant.

SAM: Although my brand new favorite girl's name is Cassandra.

RICH: *(Stunned)* What?

SAM: Cassandra. Isn't it a beautiful name? A little exotic—I know you like the exotic ones.

RICH: What do you mean by that?

SAM: You know what I mean.

RICH: I don't. I don't know what you mean at all.

SAM: You like the exotic names. Cassandra's kind of exotic. Don't you think?

RICH: No, I don't.

SAM: I do. Very classy. Very European.

RICH: Why are you saying all this?

SAM: Saying all what?

RICH: This. All this stuff about Cassandra.

SAM: *(A little taken aback)* I like the name, Rich. I came across it recently and it struck me as a really beautiful name. One that you might like.

RICH: Well I don't.

SAM: Obviously. Didn't realize you'd freak out about it. As you always say, just let it bubble under for a while and see what you think.

RICH: I don't like it. It's just not a name I like. *(Pause)* Where did you come across it?

SAM: On our Caller ID.

RICH: At home?

SAM: No—at the pay phone over there. I was looking for a phone number and it scrolled by. Cassandra something. The name just struck me.

RICH: When was the call?

SAM: I have no idea. I just noticed the name. It's really unique. Why?

RICH: No reason. I hadn't seen it the last time I checked the Caller ID. It's definitely a name you would notice.

SAM: I figured if you like Ruby and Roxy, you might like Cassandra.

RICH: *(Looking closely at her)* I guess I might.

*Nurse 2 enters.*

NURSE 2: Samantha?

SAM: Right here.

NURSE 2: Follow me please.

SAM: *(To RICH)* Let's see how the little nipper's doing.

*RICH gets up slowly and follows SAM. Fade to black.*

## SCENE FIVE

*RICH and SAM'S apartment. SAM is getting ready to go
out; RICH is sitting on the couch, flipping through the TV
channels, beer in hand.*

SAM: I just hope the whole night isn't too much of a downer.
Every time I talk to Rebecca lately she sounds so depressed.

RICH: Yeah, well, what does she expect?

SAM: I think it's reasonable to expect your husband to actually—

RICH: Soon to be ex-husband.

SAM: To at least be mature enough to have an adult conversation.

RICH: She knew when she married him that Andy is not your
poster child for the mature male.

SAM: But that's no excuse for how he's been acting about all this.

RICH: What's he supposed to do? Forget about it? Forget that she
was sleeping with this guy for like six months and lying about it
to his face? She may still be sleeping with him for all we know.

SAM: She says she isn't anymore.

RICH: She also said she wasn't sleeping with him in the first
place.

SAM: I know Andy's your friend, Rich, but we've known Rebecca a
long time now. She's really hurting in all this, too. It's not just
Andy. Though he carries on as if it was.

RICH: And David. I told you the story about the kid we knew
growing up—

SAM: Yeah, and it's really sad, but David has a mother, too. And
the way Andy's dealing with all this is certainly being read by

David. Rebecca told me the other day that he's started to ignore her sometimes when she's talking to him.

RICH: I'm not saying Andy's handling this the best way he could, or the way I would, or the way most reasonable people would. But Rebecca did a really terrible, really shitty thing to him. So it's hard to feel sympathy for her.

SAM: It's not the most horrible thing in the world, Rich. It happens to a lot of couples—

RICH: You don't think it's a horrible thing? To have an—?

SAM: And a lot couples get through it. No, I don't think it's the most horrible thing in the world.

RICH: To have an affair for six months? And lie about it when you get caught?

SAM: I don't think it's a great thing to do either, Rich. There's nothing good about it. But it's not like she killed someone.

RICH: *(Pause)* Of course it isn't. But she lied to him, Sam. Every day. For six months. Getting into bed with him, kissing him goodbye in the morning, going to family events—it was a lie every minute. And then when Andy figured out something was going on, she continued to lie to his face for months.

SAM: Look. You're missing my point. What Rebecca did was wrong. She knows what she did was wrong; we all know it was wrong. And she feels terrible about it, Rich—whether you want to believe her or not. Rebecca having this affair was so much more about her, and they way she feels about her life, than it was about Andy. Although their relationship certainly played a part of it.

RICH: *(Annoyed)* So Andy should just forgive and forget, huh?

SAM: Ultimately, yes. If he can.

RICH: He'll never forget, that's for sure.

SAM: And that's fine. He probably shouldn't forget it. Rebecca should never forget it either. It's damaged their relationship severely. Whether or not Andy can ever forgive Rebecca is the heart of it. I mean, look at your parents—

RICH: Look at them. They're divorced.

SAM: But it was like what? Two or three affairs later that your dad finally stopped being able to forgive?

RICH: *(Testily)* So every marriage should get a few affair mulligans? One or two freebies before the shit really hits the fan? What's the ruling on one-night stands versus protracted affairs?

SAM: *(Staring him down)* Cut the sarcasm, Rich.

RICH: But aren't you saying that Andy should be forgiving because it's only one little affair?

SAM: No, that's *not* what I'm saying. What I'm saying is that adult people who supposedly love each other need to work out major problems like this together. Not act like some petulant little brat—

RICH: He's got a right to—

SAM: I'm not finished—stop interrupting me. What pisses me off about the way Andy's acting is that it reminds me of some five-year-old kid who isn't getting his way. He's a grown man, for chrissake. When he was here last weekend I wanted to slap that self-pitying pout right off his whiny face.

RICH: He's always been—

SAM: I said stop interrupting me, O.K.? I'm not finished.

RICH: Excuse me. I was agreeing with—

SAM: If he wants to be pissed at Rebecca, fine. I understand. He can stay angry till he dies for all I care. But at this point, just be civil. Be an adult. Be a grown man. Don't teach your son that treating the people around you like shit is O.K.—no matter what has happened. He supposedly loves Rebecca, right? *(Pause, waiting for an answer)* Right?

RICH: *(Startled)* That was a question to me? Yes. He supposedly loves Rebecca.

SAM: Then the least he could do is muster a modicum of respect for the woman he supposedly loves and be civil. That's all I'm saying.

RICH: *(Waiting. Then)* Is that all?

SAM: *(Sitting, tired)* For now. Yeah. I'm sure I'll be able to work up more later, but that's about all the energy I've got now.

RICH: Then let me ask you a question. What if one of us had an affair?

SAM: Had?

RICH: Has—future tense. What if one of us has an affair? A one-night stand, let's say.

SAM: I guess it would depend on—

RICH: Wouldn't you be furious?

SAM: Of course I would. And in this condition, seven months pregnant, I'd probably strangle you with my bare hands.

RICH: So what about this civility thing?

SAM: They're not mutually exclusive, Rich. I would be furious, of course, but the sheer anger would eventually die down and I'd have to really assess what was wrong with our relationship that might have brought this about. But I'd at least be civil throughout.

RICH: And you'd be forgiving?

SAM: Probably. Part of it would depend on you. I mean, if you met some little chippy and decided that she was the one you wanted to be with for the rest of your life and you left me, well, there isn't much I could do but be furious. And sad. But if it was a one-time thing, despite how angry I might be, I'd eventually forgive you. And maybe even forget it.

RICH: I couldn't.

SAM: Forgive me?

RICH: No. Forget.

SAM: What about you? What if I came home one night and told you I was having an affair?

RICH: When you're 8 months pregnant? I'd have to tip my hat to—

SAM: Very funny.

RICH: I don't know. I mean…I'd be furious, of course. My head would probably explode. That's how pissed I'd be. I don't know, Sam. What you said all sounds so reasonable, so "adult," but I don't know how I would take it. Maybe if it was a one-night stand kind of thing I'd feel less murderous. I'd probably freak out like Andy is and then—

SAM: No you wouldn't. You're much too reasonable to carry on like Andy is. Not enough self-pity.

RICH: Oh I can muster self-pity alright.

SAM: I'm guessing you'd react more like your dad did than anything. You watched him go through it with your mom.

RICH: I always wondered why he wasn't angrier. 'Cause I think there would be a real anger element for me.

SAM: Did you ever ask him why?

RICH: I never did. I always kind of thought of it as a weakness in him.

SAM: That he didn't get angry about your mom's affairs?

RICH: Yeah. In general, really. He was never one to get really pissed off or yell or anything like that.

SAM: That's because he's a genuinely thoughtful, reasonable man.

RICH: I've never told him I felt that way. He'd get on Chris and me when we'd fly off the handle or get really angry about something and I'd always think it was because he was weak in that way. Especially when I was teenager. I had a bit of a temper. So to me it was just him trying to make me be passive like he was.

SAM: There's some teen logic for you.

RICH: It's total teen logic. Now, at this point in my life, I see it differently. But I still wish I would've seen him get really angry about the whole thing with my mom. It was like he had no emotion about it. Like he didn't care all that much.

SAM: I'm sure he did.

RICH: I know he did, but for a guy who's usually so effusive about everything it was one area where sheer anger was warranted and he never showed anything even remotely like it. I can assure you that if you told me you were having an affair, my anger would show loud and clear.

SAM: I'll call you on the phone then.

RICH: But I've thought about it.

SAM: *(Suspiciously)* About what?

RICH: About you having an affair, and what I might do. I mean, with this thing going on with Andy and Rebecca, I'm sure everyone around them has thought about it.

SAM: That's true. I've thought about what I would do if you had an affair. And no, I personally haven't thought about having an affair. *(Pause)* Yet.

RICH: What do you mean yet?

SAM: *(Hoisting herself from the couch)* Nothing, Rich. I was trying to make a joke.

RICH: Oh. O.K.

SAM: But like so many things lately, you didn't take it in the spirit it was intended.

RICH: What do you mean by that?

SAM: *(Turning to face him)* You've seemed a little touchy about everything lately.

RICH: What do you mean touchy?

SAM: Touchy. Like a pregnant woman. The past few months you've seemed a little on edge. And distant.

RICH: I don't mean to be.

SAM: Well, you have been. But it's not an accusation.

RICH: Accusing me of what?

SAM: *(Annoyed)* Nothing. I just said I don't mean it in an accusatory way. I just figured like me you were a little freaked out about you-know-who *(pointing at her stomach)*. I know how you are when something's on your mind. You're very preoccupied. And only half way here. *(Pause)* I just wish you'd talk to me about what's going on with you.

RICH: I have been preoccupied, Sam. The baby, this whole thing with Andy and Rebecca, work has been completely insane—

SAM: Well we need to talk about this stuff more, Rich. I'm freaking out about this kid being born too, and it's coming out of my body. I've got a whole host of issues with that. And for me work has just become such a major hassle...

RICH: I know. I know. I haven't meant to be distant, but you're right—when I get overwhelmed with things I do my turtle thing. Pulling in the head to kind of maintain some form of balance–

*Loud knock on the door.*

CHRIS: *(From outside door)* Open up in there!

SAM & RICH: *(To each other, at the same time)* Chris.

CHRIS: The time has come for all good men—

*RICH opens door. CHRIS steps in, sunglasses on, beer in one hand.*

CHRIS: To rock!

SAM: *(Gathering her stuff)* Hi Chris. Love an entrance, don't you?

CHRIS: You know me too well, Sam. How's the wee being doing?

*He hugs her.*

SAM: He or she is doing well. I think you woke it up. It's kicking like crazy all of a sudden.

CHRIS: That's because it could sense its fun uncle entered the room. May I?

*He holds out his hand to feel the kicking.*

SAM: Sure. It's right over here.

CHRIS: Man...it's bouncing off the walls in there.

SAM: Tell me about it. The wall of my tiny bladder. If you'll excuse me.

*She exits to the bathroom.*

CHRIS: Ready to rock, Rich?

RICH: As ready as I'll ever be.

CHRIS: Whoa now. Don't get too pumped up. The band's not on for a few hours.

RICH: Very funny. Did you drive over here with that beer?

CHRIS: No. Bought it from a guy down the street. I parked right in front of him. A buck a beer. Right out of his trunk. Is this city great or what?

RICH: Can't beat it.

CHRIS: So did I interrupt something? You and Sam had that look like I'd—

RICH: No. Nothing major. She's going out with Rebecca tonight.

CHRIS: Ah. Fun. So why'd you give me the dirty look when you opened the door?

RICH: *(Tersely)* What did I just say?

CHRIS: That Sam's going out with—

RICH: No—I said there was nothing going on when you pounded on the door. Sorry if you thought I was giving you a dirty look...

CHRIS: No need to get snippy, princess. I just asked a simple—

SAM: *(Entering)* Snippy princess? You mean Rich or me?

CHRIS: Take a guess.

SAM: No need to. We were just talking about that very subject before you showed up.

RICH: Look, pardon me if I'm feeling a little stressed out lately. I don't need my brother and wife tag-teaming me on the subject.

SAM: *(To CHRIS)* And he tells me he isn't touchy.

CHRIS: I'm going to stay out of this one.

RICH: Thank you.

SAM: (Going to RICH) And I have a whole evening of lamenting and anger to get through—can't blow my reserves here. *(Kisses RICH)* I'll see you later. Have a good time.

RICH: I'll do my best.

SAM: *(At door, to CHRIS)* Getting him good and drunk might be just the thing, doctor.

CHRIS: I am a professional. Say hi to Rebecca for me. Tell her I'm just about done having her sorry-assed husband staying at my house. They better work out something soon.

SAM: I'll give her the message. I'm sure it'll lift her spirits. See you guys.

*SAM exits.*

RICH: Andy getting to be too much?

CHRIS: That's an understatement. I told him today he had to figure out something by next week. He's driving me abso-fucking-lutely nuts.

RICH: I appreciate you helping him out. Those few days he stayed here were way too long.

CHRIS: It's not so bad having someone living in my apartment with me—it's big enough, and we don't really see all that much of each other—but it's his mopey puss dragging around the place and the Post-it notes he leaves for me—

RICH: Post-it notes?

CHRIS: Yeah. He put one on a bowl I left in the sink. Something like "Can we put this kind of stuff in the dishwasher?" or some such snotty thing. I wanted to pop him one.

RICH: He is a bit anal retentive.

CHRIS: A bit? He bought a little shoetree thing to put in my entryway for our shoes. With a Post-it note that said "For shoes!" With an exclamation point!

RICH: *(Laughing)* That's kind of funny. "For shoes!"

CHRIS: *(Laughing now as well)* What the hell did he think I was going to put in there? Just to mess with him, I left one of my bathroom towels on it.

RICH: Did he leave you a note that said "Not for towels!"— exclamation point?

CHRIS: No, but the towel was gone and back in the bathroom when I came home that night. Fie on whoever invented the Post-it note.

RICH: Wasn't that Mike Nesmith of The Monkees' mom or something like that?

CHRIS: That's Liquid Paper. Look, I know I offered him my place, and I'm certainly not going to kick him out or anything, but it just seems like he's getting a little too comfortable, you know what I mean? I figured a couple of weeks maybe, and then he'd have something figured out. But it's over a month now...

RICH: You're doing a good deed though, Chris.

CHRIS: I know, but I'm not feeling the full return—any return, really—on the good deed. Plus, he's always so bummed out.

RICH: Yeah, he's really deep into it.

CHRIS: I've taken him out a few times, like to see a movie, or we went to dinner one night and he got absolutely blasted. But it's just a short-lived distraction. Everything comes back to Rebecca and David.

RICH: At least he's not missing so much work. I thought he was on his way to getting canned for missing so much time. That would kill him—losing his job.

CHRIS: Not while he's living at my place. I'm not charging him rent or anything, but the thought of him sitting in my living room weeping and drinking my good scotch—

RICH: Does he do that a lot?

CHRIS: Which? The weeping or the drinking of my good scotch?

RICH: I guess both.

CHRIS: Some of the former, and only once of the latter. I put a stop to that shit real quick.

RICH: That must be awkward.

CHRIS: Not really—I just told him not to touch any of the scotch on the top—

RICH: I meant the weeping.

CHRIS: I knew what you meant. He doesn't do it that often. He may be bawling his eyes out whenever I'm gone, but when I'm around he seems to keep it to a minimum. But that wouldn't really bother me. The guy's personal life is pretty fucked up right now. He has full weeping rights I think.

RICH: True. He wasn't much of a crier when we were kids.

CHRIS: I don't remember. You were enough of a crier for the lot of us.

RICH: Bullshit.

CHRIS: Bullshit nothing. I don't know how many times when we were kids you'd end up crying about something and I'd catch heat from mom—even if I had nothing to do with it. "You're supposed to watch out for your little brother."

RICH: You can't pin that on me. That was mom.

CHRIS: I know, I know. But it was always implied that I should've been looking out for you somehow.

RICH: Sorry to have been such a burden.

CHRIS: Apology not accepted. However, I *will accept* dinner as partial payment.

RICH: *(Grabbing his coat to leave)* Sushi?

CHRIS: I need something heartier to soak up the copious beers you'll be buying me tonight. Again—as partial payment. How 'bout El Tio? It's right down the street from the club.

RICH: *(Opening door, checking for keys)* I can do Mexican. Grab a cab?

CHRIS: A cab? With the guy selling beer right outside your building? Let's walk—it's a beauty night.

RICH: *(At door)* That's quite a hike, Chris.

CHRIS: *(Exiting, patting RICH on the stomach)* The exercise will be good for one of us.

RICH: *(Closing door)* Now you're looking out for my health?

CHRIS: *(From behind closed door)* A big brother's job is never done.

*Fade to black.*

## SCENE SIX

*SAM and RICH's apartment, many hours later. We hear the beep of the answering machine and "You have one new message." As the stage illuminates, we see RICH leaning near the machine, a bit woozy, listening to the message.*

REBECCA: *(Inebriated)* Hi, Rich. It's Rebecca. Nothing to worry about here. I just wanted to let you know that Sam is crashed on our couch—on my couch. It's about 12:30 right now. We started watching a movie late and she just zonked out and I didn't want to wake her. I know I talked her ear off tonight. She probably just passed out from sheer exhaustion. If she wakes up soon, I'll make sure she gets a cab home. I'd take her home myself, but I'd rather not wake David this late and drag him out of bed. So I'm just going to let her sleep. *(Pause)* She's such a great friend, Rich. She really is. *(Sounding a little weepy)* I really miss both of you, Rich. I know you think I'm really horrible and a total bitch, but...but I'm not. I really wish this wasn't my life right now. I really wish...I wish a lot of things, y'know? Anyway. I know it's just the wine talking here, but I really do miss both of you, Rich. I really do. And I'm so excited for you and Sam and the baby. I think it's just great. You guys are going to be such great parents...

*Offstage, we hear the flush of the toilet, and the opening of the bathroom door.*

CHRIS: Oh that felt good. I think my kidneys shrunk about—

RICH: *(Sloppily)* Shhhhh!

CHRIS: *(Quietly)* Who is it?

RICH: *(Finger still at lips, whispering)* Rebecca. Drunk Rebecca.

REBECCA: *(Continuing)*...sure, everyone *thinks* they're going to be great parents, of course, but I know you two really *are* going to be great at it. God knows I try to be a good mother, and Andy's... Andy's a pretty good dad overall. I guess I'm a better mother than wife at this point, huh? I know what you're thinking. I know.

*REBECCA sobs slightly.*

REBECCA: O.K. Enough. Listen to me—I've talked at Sam for hours and now I'm talking your ear off on your answering machine. I need to just shut up and sleep. So Sam's safe here with me. No need to worry. Take care, Rich. Bye. *(About to hang up and then)* Oh—so I don't forget. Tell your brother he is a saint—an absolute *saint*—for letting Andy stay with him this long. He can be a real pain in the ass to live with, Rich. As you know. As *I* know. So Chris must be an absolute saint to let him stay so long. Really. Don't forget to tell him for me, O.K.? Goodnight, Rich.

*The phone is hung up clumsily.*

CHRIS: She sounded toasted.

RICH: *(Walking to kitchen)* No shit. What a bitch.

CHRIS: I think she was pretty much right on with the saint stuff.

RICH: *(From kitchen)* Saint Christopher. Wasn't he the patron saint of fuck-ups?

CHRIS: No. He was the patron saint of dealing with assholes.

RICH: *(Returns to living room with a beer)* Very funny.

CHRIS: *Another* night cap? You had like five before we left the bar.

RICH: What? Are counting my drinks?

CHRIS: I stopped counting a couple—

RICH: Fuck you. What are you, mom now?

CHRIS: Hey—chill out, Rich. You've been acting belligerent all night.

RICH: No I haven't.

CHRIS: *Yes.* You *have.* You acted like a jerk at the show—

RICH: Whatever. *(Sitting down on the couch)* Saint Christopher.

*CHRIS, eyeing RICH, walks toward the couch.*

CHRIS: What's up with you, Rich? Seriously?

RICH: Nothing. Nothing—ALL RIGHT! Stop asking me that. You've asked me that about a million times tonight.

CHRIS: I ask because there's something going on with you. I know it. I can tell, Rich. I can always tell with you.

RICH: Bullshit. Your radar or whatever is picking up a bad signal this time.

*The brothers sit in silence, CHRIS staring at RICH as if expecting an answer. RICH becomes progressively more uncomfortable.*

RICH: *(Trying to lighten the situation)* Man, can you believe that message she left? I should save the tape and play it for her sometime—

CHRIS: Why do you seem so obsessed with this Andy and Rebecca thing?

RICH: Obsessed? Ha! I only mentioned it because of the message Rebecca left. You heard her. She sounded—

CHRIS: I'm not talking about the message. You've talked about their situation at least a half dozen times this evening, Rich. In the cab on our way back here you brought it up again.

RICH: Sorry. It's just kind of a big deal going on with one of our friends. And hell—Andy's driving you nuts living at your place.

CHRIS: But why are you so mad at Rebecca?

RICH: I'm not "so mad at Rebecca."

CHRIS: Then why did you keep referring to her as "that bitch Rebecca."

RICH: Look, she's married to my oldest friend in the world and she was fucking some other guy for the past six months. I think that's kind of a bitchy thing to do, don't you?

CHRIS: Did you have an affair with Rebecca?

RICH: WHAT?

CHRIS: You heard me.

RICH: Are you fucking nuts?

CHRIS: I'm asking because you are obviously really pissed off at her about—

RICH: That's unbelievable, Chris. I wouldn't fuck Rebecca with your dick.

CHRIS: *(Stunned)* That is completely uncalled for, Rich.

RICH: C'mon, bro. That's a great fucking line.

CHRIS: Not in this instance, Rich. It's a great fucking line when you don't know or don't care about the fuckee or the stand-in dick. But not here. Not when you're talking about a friend's wife or—

RICH: Lighten up, Saint Christopher. It was a joke. You know— break the tension a little bit?

CHRIS: But I don't want to break the tension, Rich. I don't want to give you an easy out. I don't want to let you off the hook with an ill-timed—albeit classic—dick joke. I don't want to let you—

RICH: *(Angrily)* What is it that you want then?

CHRIS: I want you to tell me what the fuck is going on with you lately. What's *really* going on—?

RICH: Nothing. Nothing nothing nothing nothing NOTHING. What don't you understand about nothing?

CHRIS: I understand you're bullshitting me. That's what I understand. For the past few months you've been acting—

RICH: Nothing, Chris. NOTHING. Don't you get?

CHRIS: Were you somehow involved with Rebecca, Rich?

RICH: *(Terse, nearly fuming)* I said NO!

CHRIS: Were you the affair?

RICH: NO!

*He charges at CHRIS and attempts to grab him but loses his balance and falls awkwardly into him. After a brief pause, RICH pushes away from CHRIS.*

RICH: No. You asshole. No.

*CHRIS remains standing in the same place. RICH turns to the couch and sits. He puts his head in his hand.*

CHRIS: *(Quietly)* You can tell me, Rich. You know you can always tell me.

*Pause. He notices RICH'S shoulders are shaking.*

CHRIS: Oh man, Rich. Were you the affair?

RICH: *(Head still in hands, shaking no.)* No. *(Pause)* Not with Rebecca.

CHRIS: But there was an affair?

*RICH shakes his head 'yes' with his head still in his hands.*

CHRIS: Sam had an affair?

*RICH shakes his head 'no' with his head still in his hands.*

CHRIS: Oh. *(Pause)* O.K.

*CHRIS crosses to kitchen. We hear water running. He returns to living room with a glass of water. He sets the water on the coffee table in front of RICH and moves his beer away. CHRIS sits near RICH on the couch.*

CHRIS: Talk to me, Rich.

RICH: *(Head still in hands)* I can't. I can't, Chris.

CHRIS: Of course you can, Rich. I've always been the one you can talk to. And I'm guessing this is one you really need to talk about. *(Pause)* Here. Take a drink.

*RICH parts his hands and sees the beer and glass of water on the coffee table. He reaches for the beer. Chris snatches it before RICH can grab it.*

CHRIS: That one's mine.

*RICH drops his hands from his face, shaking his head slightly. He is still unable to look at CHRIS.*

RICH: Jerk.

*RICH picks up the glass of water, downing the entire glass.*

CHRIS: So what happened, Rich?

RICH: *(Falls back into couch, head still bowed)* It's bad, Chris. It's really, really bad.

CHRIS: It's never as bad as you think, Rich.

RICH: This is really fucking bad.

CHRIS: O.K. So what happened?

*RICH continues staring at the floor, unable to look at Chris.*

CHRIS: *(Reaches over to RICH and puts his hand on his shoulder.)* Rich. Get it out, man. So it's really bad. Fine. I'm not going to pass any judgments. You know that. *(Pause)* So you had an affair—that's not so bad, Rich. It's not like you killed someone, for chrissake.

*RICH covers his face with hands again and slowly bends forward, his head at his knees. CHRIS keeps his hand on RICH'S shoulder. Suddenly, RICH stands and walks to another part of the room.*

RICH: Remember the night I blew off the concert?

CHRIS: Yeah.

RICH: I wasn't sick.

CHRIS: I know.

RICH: And I knew you knew.

CHRIS: You wouldn't miss that show for the world.

RICH: Right. Right.

CHRIS: So is that the night this thing started?

RICH: It didn't start anything. It was that one night.

*Pause. RICH finally looks at Chris.*
RICH: And it *wasn't* Rebecca.

CHRIS: I kinda got that.

RICH: Asshole.

CHRIS: Fair enough. Who was it?

RICH: No one you know. No one I even know. You know

Gourmand—that coffee shop by my office?

CHRIS: Yeah.

RICH: That's where it started. Or where this one night started. I went in to grab a cup of coffee after work. To go. I should've just got it to go like I planned.

CHRIS: "The best laid plans..."

RICH: So as I'm doctoring up my coffee I see this incredibly striking woman sitting near the front window. She appears to be alone, has a bunch of books and notebooks on the table in front of her. And I can't stop staring at her. A table right near where she's sitting is open, and it's like I couldn't stop myself.

CHRIS: I know the feeling.

RICH: I sit down with my coffee, making a little bit of a racket about it to try to catch her attention. She glances over at me with a generic friendly smile, and she's even more stunning up close. So I settle in, figuring I'll kill a little time and try not to get caught blatantly staring at her. She's pouring over what looks like a textbook and a bunch of notes, and it dawns on me—I've got our book club book in my bag. *(Crosses to bookshelf, pulls out book, and crosses to CHRIS)* So I pull this out and start pretending to read.

CHRIS: *(Taking book)* Ah. *A Moveable Feast.* Hemingway. Great book. Romantic book.

RICH: So I find out. And it was a great read.

CHRIS: And she's a Hemingway fan?

RICH: I guess. But after about 10 minutes of reading the same couple of sentences over and over again, eyeballing her over the top of the page, she notices the book and comments on it. "That's a fantastic book." In this really foxy voice. Foreign sounding. I say I'm reading it for a book club, she says something about us

Americans and our book club craze-

CHRIS: Where was she from?

RICH: Everywhere, it seems. Italian diplomat father, Egyptian mother.

CHRIS: Very exotic.

RICH: Exactly. The exact word I keep coming back to. Exotic. I found myself flirting like a fiend with her. And I don't really even know why, Chris. I still don't. She was just this really attractive, striking, fascinating woman. Young woman.

CHRIS: How young?

RICH: Mid-20s? She's here doing pre-med work at University of Chicago, she's traveled all around the world, super-smart, very witty, sexy voice—

CHRIS: Aside from the pre-med and all the travel, you could be describing—

RICH: Sam. I know, I know. But this was something else. Something completely...else.

CHRIS: It was *someone* else.

RICH: Yes. That was part of it. But honest, Chris, I had no designs on this woman—Cassandra. Her name's Cassandra. I had no master plan on this. When we started talking, and joking, and flirting, I honestly thought it was just fun. I remember thinking while I was going on that I'd forgotten how much fun flirting can be.

CHRIS: And you don't think that something might—

RICH: No—not at all. In fact, I recall thinking at the time that were I still single, I would be really interested in pursuing this woman. Later, after we'd left the coffee shop and were having dinner—

CHRIS: So you two had dinner?

RICH: Yes. I was still planning on going to the concert with you. I'm having dinner with this woman and I'm thinking to myself, "Man, this is so wild. I can't even believe I'm doing this. Wait until I tell Chris about this." It was like a test—like I was testing myself.

CHRIS: To see how far you would go?

RICH: Kind of. But at this point I honestly had no intention of sleeping with her. I kept an eye on my watch and kept figuring how long it would take me to get home, get changed, and get over to the club in time to meet you. But then she started asking me about my personal life. She said something like "I'm surprised you're not married" or something like that.

CHRIS: Did she see your wedding ring?

RICH: I wasn't wearing it. I'd taken it in the week before to have it resized.

CHRIS: Puffing up are you?

RICH: *Totally* separate subjects. But when she said that, I realized that as far as she knew, I was this single guy showing obvious interest in her. I mean, I knew I wasn't wearing my wedding ring, and I knew that she had no other reason to think anything else. But it hit me that she was buying all this from me. She had no idea that I was pretending to be someone that I'm not.

CHRIS: You didn't make up like a whole new life or anything weird like that, did you?

RICH: Not at all. I should have, as it turns out, but no—I wasn't "Steve" the tennis pro or "Zack" the investment banker.

CHRIS: Zack—even the name sounds jerky.

RICH: Exactly. The point is, to her, to Cassandra, I was just this single guy who was obviously interested in her. And she was obviously interested in me.

CHRIS: And that's what sealed the deal.

RICH: *(Pause)* Yeah. That was part of it. A big part of it. *(Pause)* You know that look women give you when they're interested—really interested?

CHRIS: I know it well, my friend.

RICH: Yeah, right. It's not just a look, it's a whole...energy. A whole kind of electric energy. There's almost a smell to it, you know?

CHRIS: I do. I know exactly what you mean. And that's when sleeping with her became an option?

RICH: Yes. A real possibility. At one point she grabbed my hand and said something—I have *no* idea what she said—but that touch just set me off. *(Pause)* It was the most exciting physical contact I'd had in a long time. And I don't mean anything against Sam, but it was—

CHRIS: It was different. It was a totally new skin touching you.

RICH: Exactly. And it made me feel...confident? I don't know if that's the right word. It made me feel exceptional. Like here I was with this really exciting woman who wanted me. Physically. And that desire was...being desired like that made me really...

CHRIS: Horny.

RICH: Not just that. I mean, obviously horny. Of course. But it was like I saw an adventure—a little cul-de-sac of an adventure on this road I seem to be on.

CHRIS: With Sam?

RICH: With my life. It's not even so much about Sam. This whole thing's really not much about Sam when I think about it.

CHRIS: I'm guessing Sam won't agree. Or doesn't agree—does she know yet?

RICH: Are you kidding me? Tell your pregnant wife that you've had an affair?

CHRIS: I have to ask: was Sam pregnant yet?

RICH: No. I mean, yes. But we didn't know. *I* didn't know yet. It wasn't until a few days later that we took the pregnancy test.

CHRIS: I guess technically you *were* pregnant when this happened.

RICH: *Technically*, yes. But I didn't know we were pregnant.

CHRIS: But you guys had been trying, right?

RICH: For a while.

CHRIS: You were trying to become a father.

RICH: *(Annoyed)* But it's a key point: I didn't *know* we were pregnant. We'd had no luck for a long time, some false alarms—

CHRIS: But Sam's not going to be too negotiable on the technicality of it.

RICH: I know. *(Pause)* I know.

CHRIS: Was the fact that you two were trying to start a family part of this?

RICH: It all was. That's what I was starting to say—it's like I'm headed down this well-worn, perfectly safe, what's-expected-of-me kind of path. Graduate college, get a good job, get married to your college sweetheart, advance in your job, buy a condo, have some kids, move to the suburbs, buy a fucking mini-van, cultivate a respectable beer belly—it's like I can see the whole fucking thing right down to my kids thanking people for coming to my funeral and my grandkids arguing over my record collection. Clear as day I can see it.

CHRIS: And it's not what you want?

RICH: I don't even know. That's the messed up part, Chris. That doesn't sound like such a bad life, y'know?

CHRIS: And sleeping with this woman was going to do ...what?

RICH: I don't know. Nothing, probably. Fuck things up with me and Sam, certainly. *(Pause)* But it was my decision, y'know? I had a choice. And I made the choice.

CHRIS: But you've been making choices all along this road you've seen—

RICH: I know. It's my life. I've made it. But it's as if the decisions I've made so far have set in motion something that I have less and less control of. Something with its own kinetic energy that I just hang onto now for the rest of the ride.

CHRIS: Now you're someone's husband, soon you'll be someone's dad.

RICH: I wanted to be someone's husband. I *want* to be someone's husband. And I want to be someone's dad. But it's like quicksand, y'know? The farther you go into it, the deeper it sucks you in.

CHRIS: And you don't want to get sucked in?

RICH: I don't want to drown. I don't want to wake up one day 20 years from now and think, "Where the fuck did I go? Where was I all this time? Who am I?"

*Silence. CHRIS sits on the couch, watching RICH, who is deep in thought, obviously realizing what he has said.*

CHRIS: From everything I've seen, and been told, that's the whole struggle, isn't it? *(Waiting for a response from RICH.)* Dad jokes about all those years being a blur of driving us from one place to another and trying to find time to enjoy an uninterrupted thought. I think that's just part of the whole family, fatherhood deal. *(Waiting again for a response.)* I wouldn't know, of course, but there's got to be some kind of payoff. I mean, people keep having kids, right? Look at Andy. I think he's way more broken up about his son being a divorce kid than he is about actually getting a divorce. And he's probably someone who shouldn't have had any kids anyway—talk about your selfish bastard. But man, he loves that David like crazy. *(Looking for some kind of response from RICH)* Can I ask you something?

RICH: *(Looking at CHRIS)* What?

CHRIS: Are you going to tell Sam?

RICH: I don't know. *(Pause)* Dad says I shouldn't.

CHRIS: Dad knows about this?

RICH: I had to talk to someone about it.

CHRIS: What am I? Chopped liver?

RICH: No. It's just different. Dad's so…accepting. He was safe. I knew what your reaction would be.

CHRIS: What reaction? I haven't reacted one way or another.

RICH: I appreciate that. But I know you, Chris. Mr. Honesty. Wait—that was "Saint" Christopher, wasn't it? I know exactly what you think I should do.

CHRIS: Tell Sam about it.

RICH: Precisely. I didn't even have to ask.

CHRIS: I understand you don't want to tell her now. But you have to, Rich. It's the only way.

RICH: But what's it going to accomplish?

CHRIS: Accomplish? It's not a matter of accomplishing anything. It's about being honest with the person you love the most. And yourself.

RICH: Honesty—I know, Chris. But this is so much more complicated than...there's a lot at stake here. And it's not just a matter of timing. When's the right time to tell her?

CHRIS: When's the right time for anyone to tell his spouse he had an affair?

RICH: Never. The reason I said the thing about what would it accomplish is because when I talked to Dad about the whole—

CHRIS: He really said he didn't think you should tell Sam about this?

RICH: I was as surprised as you. But his point was this: what was it going to mean to Sam? You know? How was it going to affect her? I'm not having an affair with this woman—it was a one-time mistake.

CHRIS: But you've always said that you and Sam have a really open and honest relationship. That it was a basic value you both shared—

RICH: We do, Chris. And that's why this is killing me. If I don't tell her, it would be the first time either of us harbored such a massive lie. And if I do tell her...

CHRIS: *(Jumping on the opening)* It'll suck and be painful and awkward and she's going to be furious at you for a while, but at least you won't have to spend the rest of your life with this bullshitty little one-night stand eating away at you. I mean, the longer you put it off, the less likely you'll ever tell her. Do you wait until after the baby's born? And if that long, why not wait a few more months, until she's back at work and blah blah blah. Do you tell her the truth a year from now? Two years from now?

RICH: I know. I KNOW. It's fucked up, Chris. I know I should tell her. But I don't know that I can. Tell her the truth. *(Pause)* I keep coming back to what Dad said, about what telling Sam would really accomplish.

CHRIS: I'm still surprised that he said such a thing. After what he went through with Mom.

RICH: I was stunned too. But he told me this *really* messed up story about this thing he started doing with our old neighbor—

CHRIS: Mrs. Anderson? And the window?

RICH: *(Physically stunned)* He told you about that?

CHRIS: Yeah. Years ago.

RICH: Dad said he'd never told anyone about Mrs. Anderson.

CHRIS: Maybe he forgot he told me. But he didn't tell Mom, I know that.

RICH: That's why he told me the whole perverse story, to make the point that he never told Mom about it. Because he didn't see what good it would do.

CHRIS: But that's totally different, Rich. You had sex with someone. It's a totally different thing.

RICH: I know it is.

CHRIS: That's actual physical contact.

RICH: I know.

CHRIS: It's a completely different violation of marriage.

RICH: I know, Chris.

CHRIS: So how can you equate the way Dad dealt with this weird visual fantasy kind of thing with what you did?

RICH: *(Silent, looking down)* I can't. *(Pause)* But I know it'll just...

CHRIS: Just what?

RICH: I know it'll just crush Sam. It'll completely change everything.

*Pause. RICH slumps down into the couch, again covering his face with his hands.*

RICH. She'll hate what I've done.

CHRIS: *(Going to RICH on the couch)* Sam loves you, Rich. She loves you like crazy. She'll be really pissed off at you—deservedly so—but she's not like Andy. She's rational. Even if she doesn't react rationally at first, she'll work through her anger and get to a place where she can think straight about the whole thing. I know Sam. She's not some simpering woman who's going to let her life be crushed by a passing infidelity. She's too strong for that.
*Pause. He puts his arm around RICH'S shoulders.*

CHRIS: Just be honest with her, Rich. Tell her the truth.

RICH: *(Muffled, hands still covering face)* I can't tell her the truth.

CHRIS: Of course you can. Just tell her—

*RICH's head snaps up, tears in his eyes. He stares straight at CHRIS.*

RICH: I CAN'T tell her the truth. The WHOLE truth.

CHRIS: Why not?

*RICH stands and walks away.*

RICH: Because it's nothing I want her to know about me.

CHRIS: *(Suspiciously)* What do you mean the "whole" truth, Rich?

RICH: Exactly that—the whole truth. Everything that happened.

CHRIS: Did you tell Dad the whole truth?

RICH: No.

CHRIS: *(Standing, turning to RICH)* Did you tell me the whole truth? Here? Tonight?

RICH: *(Staring at CHRIS, shaking his head)* No.

*The brothers stand looking at each other, CHRIS waiting, RICH trying to figure out what—if anything—to say.*

CHRIS: Just tell me, Rich. What's the whole truth?

RICH: *(Staring directly at CHRIS)* She's pregnant. *(Pause) Was* pregnant.

CHRIS: *(Not dropping RICH'S stare)* And you don't mean Sam.

RICH: No. I don't mean Sam.

CHRIS: Wow.

RICH: *(Moving a little toward CHRIS)* Now do you see why I can't tell Sam? Why I can't tell her the whole truth?

CHRIS: It's certainly a lot more...complicated.

RICH: Complicated? It's a total fucking mess is what it is.

CHRIS: That too.

RICH: So I think to myself, I should tell Sam about sleeping with Cassandra. I should be totally honest with her about that. But what if she asks me something like, oh, I don't know—did I use any protection? Then do I say, No, honey, because I'm a total moron and I—

CHRIS: *(Suddenly)* You are a total moron, Rich. What the hell were you thinking? In this day and age? Even teenagers know to use—

RICH: I know, Chris. It was amazingly dumb. On both our parts.

CHRIS: Have you gotten tested?

RICH: Yes. And I'll get tested again in a few months. But you see? This is what I've been dealing with? How—*what* version of "the truth" do I tell Sam? Do I tell her the 'I had unprotected sex and got a woman pregnant' version? While we were trying to have a baby? And tell her this when she's eight months pregnant with our child? Or do I tell her the 'I had a meaningless one-night stand while she was out of town' version? And lie about using protection? When Sam's eight months pregnant with our child?

CHRIS: You said this woman Cassandra *was* pregnant. Does that mean you—

RICH: Yes. That's exactly what it means.

CHRIS: An abortion.

RICH: Yes. That.

CHRIS: And you know for certain that—

RICH: *(Annoyed)* Yes, Chris. I went with her. I took her home. I checked in with her until she was feeling well enough to ask me never to check in on her or call her again.

CHRIS: Just asking.

RICH: I did the right thing by her, Chris. O.K.?

CHRIS: *(Restraining himself)* O.K. O.K. Rich.

RICH: But do you see now why Dad's suggestion makes the most sense? At least to me?

CHRIS: I do see it, Rich. And I'll be completely blunt: it makes the most sense to you because you've always shied away from the really tough stuff. The uncomfortable, nasty, muddy, painfully difficult situations—you find a way to disappear. To avoid them straight-on—

RICH: Bullshit on that. I've dealt with plenty of difficult situations—

CHRIS: Difficult maybe, but not the really harsh stuff. Remember when Grandma was living with us, right before she died?

RICH: C'mon Chris—I was what? Maybe 9 years old?

CHRIS: You were 13. I was graduating high school. I know. Grandma was dying, right there in our house, and you were rarely ever even around. I think you slept over at Andy's house five nights a week.

RICH: I was a kid, Chris. I didn't know how death worked.

CHRIS: I don't hold anything against you about this, Rich. Honest. I know you were younger than I was. I'm just using it as an example. How about when Mom and Dad were getting a divorce? How many times during that whole two-year period were you back in that house? Maybe four?

RICH: More than that. Every time I went there it was like going to a wake.

CHRIS: Exactly. Because something had died in that house. I

didn't especially like going there either, but I did. Because both Mom and Dad needed us to be there for them. Not just a friendly phone call, but actually there, in that depressing house.

RICH: You know I was working a lot then. It was my first real job; I was trying to get something—

CHRIS: You lived 15 minutes from the house, Rich.

RICH: *(Annoyed)* All they ever talked about was the divorce. All those packed boxes in Mom's "half" of the house—it was depressing, O.K? I admit it. Mom would complain about what Dad was doing, Dad would make sort of passing remarks about Mom—nothing too direct, of course. It was depressing.

CHRIS: And so you disappeared. Those are the real nitty-gritty situations I'm talking about, Rich. Those are the times when people—especially your family—need you the most. When it's depressing. When they're dying. When their life is a horrible mess. When you'd rather *not* deal with the problem but you dig in and try to help because they're people that you love. So of course Dad's suggestion seems like the best answer to you—because it's *your* life that's a horrible mess right now and you'd rather avoid actually dealing with what you've done.

RICH: I *am* trying to deal with it, Chris. What the hell do you think I've been obsessing about the past five months, huh? But I can't seem to...I don't want to...

CHRIS: What? You don't want to what?

RICH: I don't want to hurt Sam. I love her. Madly, Chris. I don't want to hurt her while we're—

CHRIS: Bull SHIT. You already hurt her, Rich. She doesn't know it yet, but you've already taken care of that part. You don't want to tell her about this because you don't want her to think poorly of you. You don't want her to realize what a shit her husband can be. You don't want her to—

RICH: That's not it.

CHRIS: —to know you are fully capable of doing this really, really cliché thing—

RICH: Enough, Chris. That's not the reason.

CHRIS: *(Walking directly to RICH)* You don't want to tell her because you want everyone to like you, Rich. You've always been overly concerned with what people think of you, and you want everyone to think what a great guy you are—

RICH: *(Walking away)* Screw you, Chris.

CHRIS: Your friends, your family, the people you work with, probably even the guys who work in the mail room at your office—"Boy that Rich is a great guy, isn't he?" Right? Isn't that what this—?

RICH: Get the hell out of here.

CHRIS: This bullshit dickering around about what to do has little to do with not wanting to hurt Sam. This is about how you're going to save face and minimize damage to that great guy Rich.

RICH: *(Opening the door)* Leave please.

CHRIS: Let me assure, brother, that those of us who know you— and that means Sam— are fully aware of your imperfections. And we still love you despite them. Because of them. And now this whole mess…this will be the biggest scar yet. The biggest blemish.

RICH: Leave. Now.

CHRIS: *(Walking slowly toward the door)* And we all will think a little less of you because of it. Because it's a pretty shitty thing to do. But you know what, Rich? You'll still be my brother, and I'll still care the world for you. You'll just look a little different. A little less great, maybe.

*CHRIS stops at the open door near RICH.*

CHRIS: I'm betting Sam will see something different too. Good night, Rich.

*CHRIS closes door behind him. RICH leans against it. Suddenly— a loud knock startles RICH.*

RICH: What?

CHRIS: *(From hallway)* Open the door.

*RICH pauses, considers, then opens the door.*

RICH: What?

CHRIS: One more thing: you have to tell Sam to get tested. No matter what you end up doing about all this, whatever version you end up telling her, she has to get tested. No fucking around about it, Rich. And I swear to you if I find out it didn't happen soon, I'll tell her myself and then I will hunt you down and kick your ass. Deal? *(Extends his hand.)* Remember the last time I had to kick your ass? Huh?

*A slight glimmer of a grin flashes across RICH's face.*

RICH: All right. Deal.

*RICH shakes CHRIS' hand. Chris hold onto RICH'S hand and pulls him in for a hug.*

CHRIS: Do the right thing, Rich. Do the right thing.

*CHRIS lets go of RICH'S hand, turns, and exits, closing the door behind him. RICH leans against the door again and slowly slides down to a seated position, balled up against the door, head bowed, shoulders shaking slightly. Fade to black.*

## SCENE SEVEN

*SAM and RICH'S apartment, the following morning. SAM is lying on the couch flipping through a magazine. The TV is on; SAM occasionally looks up at the screen, and then returns to her magazine. At the sound of a door opening, SAM looks toward the hallway. At the sound of another door closing, SAM turns back to her magazine, smiling. We hear the sound of the toilet flushing, then a door opens again. SAM turns toward the hallway. Enter RICH. He is walking gingerly.*

SAM: It's...*alive.*

*RICH walks slowly toward SAM on the couch.*

RICH: No shouting, please.

SAM: Boy, you look...half dead.

*RICH leans over the back of the couch, kissing SAM.*

RICH: I feel half dead.

SAM: You smell completely dead.

RICH: *(Continuing slowly to kitchen)* Then I smell like I feel.

SAM: I take it you and Chris had a good time?

RICH: *(From kitchen)* Mostly.

SAM: When I looked in on you this morning, our bedroom smelled like a bar, so I figured it had been a successful night.

*RICH reenters from the kitchen with a two-liter bottle of soda.*

RICH: I guess it depends on how you define "success."

*He begins to drink from the bottle.*

SAM: Did you take any aspirin before you went to sleep?

RICH: Oh yeah. And I'm taking a few more now.

*He drops aspirin in his mouth and continues chugging from the bottle.*

SAM: This is such a disgusting little ritual.

RICH: *(Looking bilious)* It's a cure—not a ritual.

SAM: Whatever you call it, it's not one of your finest—

*RICH lets rip a prodigious belch.*

RICH: Oh that's great.

*He begins chugging from the bottle again. SAM jerks a little on the couch, pressing her hand to her belly.*

SAM: Well, now all of us are awake.

RICH: *(Heading toward couch)* Sorry. It's the only thing that will fuse the two halves of my skull back into place. What time is it?

SAM: Almost noon.

RICH: When did you get home?

SAM: A couple of hours ago. I woke up kind of early, and then David woke up, so we had breakfast together.

RICH: What did you have?

SAM: Cocoa Puffs.

RICH: *(Grabbing his stomach)* Ugh. Just the sound of it is making me sick.

SAM: I forgot how good they were.

RICH: I always preferred Fruit Loops.

SAM: You would.

*RICH lets out another remarkable belch.*

RICH: Oh man. Excuse me.

SAM: *(Waving her magazine)* That'd put anybody off their Fruit Loops.

RICH: I can literally feel air releasing from my pressurized brain.

SAM: How late were you guys out?

RICH: Not all that late, really. I think we got back here around 1 o'clock.

SAM: Not bad.

RICH: You should hear Rebecca's message. Sounded like somebody else might be feeling a little woozy this morning.

SAM: She was in rare form last night.

RICH: Talk your ear off?

SAM: Both ears. The wine sure did loosen her up.

RICH: How so?

SAM: She was just incredibly candid—about everything.

RICH: Her and Andy?

SAM: Her and Andy, the affair, motherhood—everything. Once she got going, it was like she couldn't stop herself.

RICH: Any highlights?

SAM: Plenty. She really doesn't want to get divorced. I think she must've said that at least 100 times. She still loves Andy, despite the way he—

RICH: Despite.

SAM: Don't start, Rich. *(Pause)* She's scared that there's no chance of reconciling with Andy.

RICH: She may be right there.

SAM: She's no longer involved with Edward. Hasn't been—

RICH: The fucker from Boston has a name?

SAM: Hasn't been involved with him for a couple of months.

RICH: Really?

SAM: That's what she says.

RICH: But doesn't she still go to Boston regularly?

SAM: She does. But he's not working on that account anymore. His decision, apparently. He was married, too.

RICH: Really?

SAM: Yes, really. According to Rebecca, they only slept together a couple of times. It was mostly flirtation and dancing around the possibility.

RICH: Do you believe her?

SAM: I do, Rich. She hasn't really been able to talk to anyone about all this, and she spilled the beans last night. It was exhausting.

RICH: So this Edward guy broke it off with her?

SAM: No. She did. I guess he started talking about maybe leaving his wife and Rebecca just cut it off.

RICH: Wow. *(Pause)* Did she say why she did it in the first place?

SAM: I asked her that. Why? And she couldn't really say. Couldn't give a solid answer. Like I said to you a couple of months ago, this whole thing was more about Rebecca herself than her marriage with Andy. She still loves him, Rich. As difficult as he is, and as shitty as he acted through all this, she's still really in love with him. Go figure.

RICH: He must've played some role in all of it though, don't you think?

SAM: Maybe. But from listening to Rebecca last night, it sounds like one of those things that just kind of happened—

RICH: That kind of stuff doesn't just "happen."

SAM: Let me finish: it happened over time. I guess Edward had been a little flirtatious with her from the first time they met. They worked closely on some initial projects, got to know each other a little more, found out they had a lot in common. Kids, difficult spouses—they both went to NYU, though he's a little younger.

RICH: A younger man?

SAM: Younger man. I hear it's just the right thing at a certain age.

RICH: That's what you hear, eh?

SAM: Anyway, it got to be this indulgent, serious flirtation for Rebecca. She said it was like a little innocent secret she had from Andy, something just for her. She's a mom, she's a wife, she's a really successful professional, she's a dutiful daughter handling most of the care for her mom—this was one thing in her life that was completely focused on her. And it just went too far.

*RICH gets up from the couch and heads toward the kitchen.*

RICH: That's an understatement. *(Another belch)* Sorry.

SAM: I think that's kind of how she views it—that it just went a bit too far. I don't think Rebecca had any emotional investment in Edward. She said as much. She says she had no intention of sleeping with him, and then it happened. And then he started talking about leaving his wife, and she wanted nothing more to do with it.

*RICH enters from the kitchen with another two-liter bottle of soda.*

RICH: Do you buy it?

SAM: Her story?

RICH: No. Her reasons. Or motivation. Whatever you want to call it.

SAM: *(Seeing two-liter bottle in his hand)* Can't you use a glass?

RICH: I guess I could.

SAM: Please. And grab me a glass too.

*RICH heads back to kitchen.*

SAM: I guess I buy her reasons. Motivations. I don't agree with what she did, of course, but I can understand how the whole thing evolved. Rebecca used a really interesting phrase last night: she referred to the "ubiquity of nets" in her life.

RICH: *(From kitchen)* Wow. That's a great line.

SAM: Obviously I don't know yet what it's like to be someone's mom, but listening to Rebecca last night, her kind of rambling explanation of how this whole affair happened and why she thinks she did it and all the different roles she's been trying to juggle... life really just gets more and more complicated, doesn't it? I mean, we're about to be parents. Talk about a complicated relationship.

*RICH appears in the doorway to the kitchen with two glasses of soda.*

RICH: That's the impression I'm getting, from everything people tell me. And from what I've seen.

SAM: *(Looking at RICH)* I know you haven't been very sympathetic to Rebecca through this whole thing, Rich, but last night really made me see her a little more clearly. So while I don't approve of what she did in any way, I guess I understand her a little better, and why she did it.

RICH: *(Still at the kitchen doorway)* Do you think it affects your opinion of her?

SAM: Meaning?

RICH: Meaning what you think about her. As a person.

SAM: *(Considering RICH'S question)* I guess it does. But it may be kind of a wash. I don't think what she did was the answer to what she was feeling about her life, so that will always define her a little bit for me. But I never really knew so much about Rebecca as I learned last night—not just about the affair, but about a whole bunch of other things going on in her life, and how she felt about them. I guess she seems more...complex? More real, maybe? Does that make any sense at all?

RICH: *(Still at kitchen doorway, almost frozen)* Kinda.

SAM: Are you going to make me hoist myself off this couch to get that drink?

RICH: Oh, sorry. Here.

*He goes to SAM on the couch, hands her the glass, and kisses her.*

SAM: Mmm. Thank you for the boozy smooch. It's like I was there last night.

*He sits on the other end of the couch, resting SAM's feet in his lap.*

RICH: So maybe I was wrong. Maybe things like that do just happen.

SAM: I don't know if things like that just happen. But in Rebecca's case, I think she found herself in this situation and simply made a really bad decision. And now she may end up paying for it dearly.

*RICH sets his glass down on the coffee table. He leans back on the couch, both hands covering his face. His breathing is audibly louder.*

SAM: *(Noticing his actions)* Rich, are you O.K.?

*No answer.*

SAM: Rich, if you're going to hork, get to the bathroom.

*No answer.*

SAM: Rich? What's the matter?

*RICH slowly sits forward, dropping his hands from his face. His eyes are glistening. He looks directly at SAM. He puts his hand on her belly. SAM puts her hand on RICH'S.*

SAM: What's the matter Rich?

RICH: *(Slowly)* Things don't just happen. *(He takes a slow, deep breath)* Sam, I have to tell you something. Something I'm so ashamed of. Something I know you don't want to hear...

*Fade to black. End of play.*

# ABOUT THE AUTHOR

**MICHAEL C. HARRIS** served as Editor of the *Illinois Entertainer,* one of the nation's longest-published entertainment magazines, from 1988-2002. Harris also hosted the rock critic talk show *Rock Tonight* with Greg Kot from 1995-1997 on WLUP in Chicago. Harris has been published in *Rolling Stone, Spin,* multiple *New Times* city publications, *Chicago* magazine, as well as the *Chicago Tribune's* Metromix site and *Red Eye* daily.

Additionally, Harris designed two writing courses for Columbia College where he has taught since 1995. He is currently a freelance writer, editor, consultant, and educator, and the author of nonfiction middle and high school books for Scholastic, Marshall Cavendish, Pearson, Penguin, and more.

Harris resides in Evanston, IL with his lovely and witty wife Carolyn and their two wonderfully vexing teenage boys Sean and Dylan. As John Lennon said, "Life is what happens to you/When you're busy making other plans."

Made in the USA
San Bernardino, CA
21 November 2015